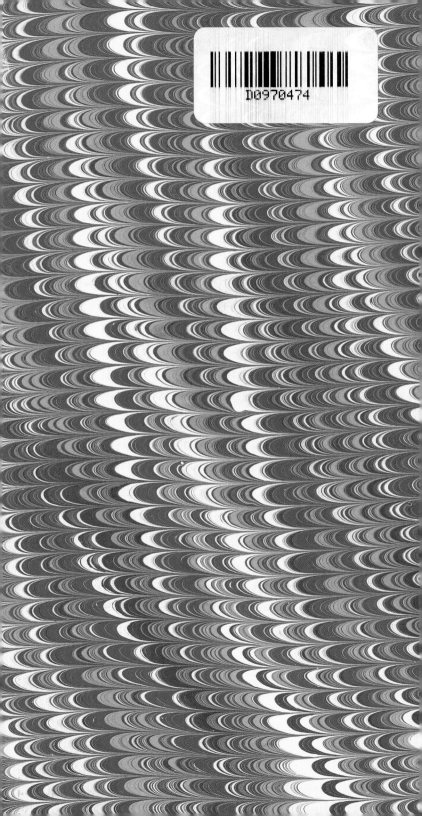
D0970474

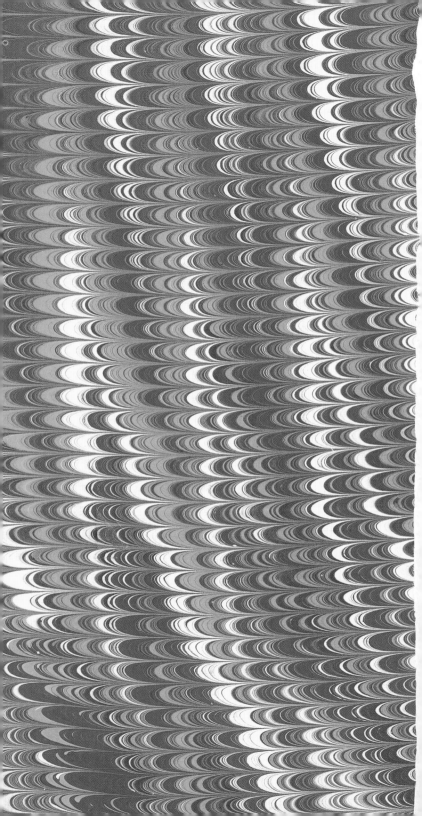

A Miscellany of
GARDEN
WISDOM

A Miscellany of
GARDEN
WISDOM

Bernard Schofield

HarperCollins*Publishers*

First published in 1991 by
HarperCollins*Publishers*

Reprinted in 1992, 1993, 1995 (twice)

Copyright © 1991 by Jackson Day Jennings Ltd/Inklink

All rights reserved. No part of this publication may be
reproduced, stored in a retrieval system, or transmitted,
in any form or by any means, electronic, mechanical,
photocopying, recording or otherwise, without the prior
written permission of the publishers.

A catalogue record of this book is available from the
British Library.

ISBN 0 00 412622 X

A Miscellany of Garden Wisdom
Compiled and arranged by Bernard Schofield
Designed by Simon Jennings
Jacket woodcut by Clare Leighton
Jacket verse by Reginald Arkell
Text edited by Albert Jackson
Picture research by Ben Jennings
Interior and back jacket illustrations by Robin Harris

Produced, edited, and designed by Inklink,
Greenwich, London, England
Published in the United States by Running Press,
Philadelphia, Pennsylvania
Typeset in ITC Garamond by Tradespools Ltd,
Frome, Somerset, England
Printed in Hong Kong by South Sea International Press

A MISCELLANY OF

GARDEN WISDOM

TABLE OF

CONTENTS

ARRANGED IN EIGHT CHAPTERS

What a man needs in gardening is a cast-iron back, with a hinge in it.

CHARLES DUDLEY WARNER 1829–1900

*I have a garden of my own,
but so with roses overgrown,
and lilies, that you would it guess
to be a little wilderness.*

ANDREW MARVELL 1621–78

I FIRST CAME UPON THE IDEA FOR THIS BOOK *while sitting in my garden one day browsing through my favorite gardening magazine. In the reader's-letters column, a woman had written in to advise on how to stop lettuces bolting, a common-enough problem among us humble amateur vegetable growers. The solution to bolting, she said, was to dig up the lettuces and then replant them; the trauma of being wrenched from the earth being enough to prohibit any further growth for several days. This advice struck me at the time as being both brilliant and absurd, and it got me thinking how there must be an enormous wealth of similar homespun tips that were once common knowledge throughout the gardening world. When I delved deeper into the subject I discovered a unique garden wisdom quite different from the usual know-how found in most books. Here was advice with its roots firmly set in an age where simplicity, ingenuity and good old practicality were the order of the day. It is supremely fitting then, I think, that as we move into the so-called New Age with its emphasis on the environment, we are discovering that* THE WAYS OF THE PAST HAVE MUCH TO TEACH US.

Bernard Schofield

BERNARD SCHOFIELD

DEDICATED TO
THE SURVIVAL OF THE
RAIN FORESTS – AND THAT
WISDOM SHALL PREVAIL.

CHAPTER ONE

SOIL AND TOIL

*The soil is rather like a bran tub –
you only get out of it what you put in.*
TRADITIONAL SAYING

A GARDENER'S RELATIONSHIP WITH *THE SOIL* and in turn that between soil and plants, are key factors in gardening. It is little short of A SPIRITUAL EXPERIENCE *to run your hands through rich, friable soil, to smell it and from it to watch things grow. For this reason* THE SOIL WE CULTIVATE MUST NOT BE ABUSED BUT LOVINGLY NURTURED, *using the rich bounty of good, natural composts and manures that are at hand, either bought in or, preferably, made ourselves. To an old-time gardener, soil science was simply inherited* WISDOM.

DOVE-COT.

THE MERITS OF DUNG

"Doves dung is ye best, the same possessth a mighty hoteness. The dung also of hen and other foules greatly commended for the sournesse, excepts ye dung of geese, ducks and other water foules. A commendation next is attributed to the Asses dung, in that the same beast for his leisurely eating, digesteth easier, and causeth the better dung. The third place is the goates dung, after this both ye Oxe and Cow dung; next the Swines dung, worthier than the Oxen or Kine. The vilest and worst of all dungs after the opinion of the Greek writers of Husbandry, is the Horse and Moiles.

The dung which men make (if the same be not mixed with the Rabbith, or dust swept out of the house) is greatly mislyked, for that by nature, it is hoter, and burneth the seedes sowne in that earth: so that this is not to be used, unlesse the grounde be barren, gravelly or verie lose sand, lacking strength in it. The mud also of running water, as the ditch or river, may bee employed instead of dung.

If no kind of dung can be purchased, then in gravelly grounds it shall be best to dung the same with chalke."

FROM *THE GARDENER'S LABYRINTH* BY THOMAS HILL BORN 1529

HOME-MADE MANURES

When it's impossible to obtain animal manure as a fertilizer there are good substitutes for farmyard or stable dung. The best "potash" manure is ash from the garden bonfire. Soot is excellent for potash, too, though both this and bonfire ash need to be left in a dry shed or outbuilding for about a year before application.

Another good all-round manure substitute comprises equal parts of spent hops, fallen leaves or leaf mold, (the latter may be available from a garden-supplies store) and "shoddy" (waste from wool mills). The ingredients should be mixed together and left for three months before you use them on the soil.

HOW TO KEEP MANURE

All animal manure should be heaped high in a dry corner of the garden and must be turned regularly to prevent it heating up. A cover, such as a sheet of corrugated iron (or plastic flooring), should be placed over the heap to protect it from rain which would wash away valuable nutrients.

MAKING MANURE GO FURTHER

Lawn mowings or straw, particularly that used as litter for poultry or rabbits, can be sandwiched in the manure heap. This significantly increases the volume of manure without decreasing it much in strength.

MOLEHILLS FOR MUSHROOMS

To grow mushrooms of perfect shape and taste, the soil in which they grow must be of better quality than normal garden soils. Many years ago, mushroom growers in country areas found that sowing the spores in soil taken from fresh molehills – "maiden soil" – produced the finest results, and moles were encouraged instead of being treated as pests.

BURY YOUR OLD BOOTS

Leather is a rich source of nutrients which once rotted down will be of benefit to the soil. So don't throw away your old shoes and boots but bury them in the garden. Make sure they are leather, though – plastic and rubber will not rot.

LEATHER FOR PEACHES

Leather was once considered an effective manure for peach trees and, many years ago, farmers were known to have traveled miles to ransack rubbish tips for discarded boots and other leather articles. The boots should be buried beneath the roots of a newly planted peach tree, or buried close to an established tree.

The cure of this ill, is not to sit still,
Or frowst with a book by the fire;
But to take a large hoe and shovel also,
And dig till you gently perspire.
FROM *THE GLORY OF THE GARDEN* BY RUDYARD KIPLING 1865–1936

CHICKEN MANURE FOR PLUMS

If you keep chickens, let them scavenge beneath your plum trees. Their droppings will increase the size of the fruit.

THE BEST LEAF MOLD

When gathering material for leaf mold, discard all fir and pine needles, cones or any evergreen leaves. This sort of material never really decays thoroughly and is apt to create fungus in the soil. Beech, oak and elm leaves make the best leaf mold. Place them in a dug-out hole in a corner of the garden, though not sheltered from the rain as this is essential for decomposition. Horticultural lime sprinkled in layers between the leaves will help to break down the material.

AMMONIA FOR LEAF MOLD

Despite their great value in the garden, decaying leaves form a fine home for many insects and their eggs, hence the necessity to sterilize the mold before it's used. Soot or horticultural lime mixed with the leaves will destroy most infestations. More effective, however, is an application of a solution of one quarter-pint of household ammonia to every gallon of water sprayed liberally over the leaf-mold heap.

DIGGING BY THE MOON

Sowing and planting according to the phases of the moon is covered in the chapter SEEDS AND SOWING. If you subscribe to this theory then it is just as important to prepare the ground at the right time. It is best to turn and work the soil when the moon is in the barren signs of Leo, Virgo, Aquarius or Gemini.

OLD DUSTBINS FOR COMPOST

When old galvanized metal dustbins finally fall to pieces it is usually the bottom that drops out, rendering them useless for their original purpose. In this state, however, they can be put to good use as compost bins. To do this, turn them upside down so that the wider top faces the ground, and the now holed bottom faces uppermost. Cut away all that remains of the bottom with a hacksaw or strong tinsnips and place the bin, still upside down, in the area for compost making. Compost material can be fed into the bin through the top and allowed to decompose for the required period of time. When required for use on the garden, the compost can be retrieved by simply lifting up the bin; it always spills out easily because the bin is widest at the bottom.

BOILING WATER FOR STERILIZING POTTING COMPOSTS

All composts have to be sterilized to create a bacteria-free growing medium in which there are no extraneous seeds. Home-made potting composts can be effectively sterilized in the following way. Fill a bucket with compost and pour over it enough boiling water to saturate all of the soil. When cool, drain off and allow it to dry in shallow boxes.

The Flattening Mill

CHAPTER TWO

SEEDS AND SOWING

This rule in gardening ne'er forget,
To sow dry and set wet.
FROM ENGLISH PROVERBS *BY JOHN RAY 1627–1705*

JOHN RAY was responsible for a great
many well-known proverbs that
are still in common usage.

FOLLOWING THE EARNEST PREPARATION OF THE SOIL
for receiving the SEED *next comes the most*
exciting period *in the garden, that of*
SOWING *There is much old* GARDEN
WISDOM *on this most satis-*
fying of tasks, a fair selection of which is presented here.

SOWING BY THE MOON

The rule here is a universal one. Always sow seed with a waxing moon, never when it's waning. The aim is to synchronize your sowing with the rhythmic powers exerted by the lunar fluctuations, being aware not just of the growing and fading moon itself, but also of its path through the zodiac. This will ensure the healthiest of plants in their season.

"The Egyptian and Greek instructions of Husbandry report, that the seeds after the bestowing, wil remain ungnawn or bitter and free of harm by creeping things in the garden, if the seeds shall be committed to the earth when the Moon possesseth her half light, or it is a quarter old."

"If the gardener mindeth to commit seeds to the earth in summer time, let the same be done in the increase of the Moon, in the moneths of July and August. In the harvest time about the middle of September, and in October, the Moon in those moneths in her first quarter; for time againe of committing seeds to the earth, let the same be done in the moneths of February and March, the Moon at those times increasing of light"

FROM *THE GARDENER'S LABYRINTH* BY THOMAS HILL BORN 1529

USING THE ZODIAC SIGNS

ARIES–*MARCH 21 TO APRIL 20*

A cardinal fire sign. Seeds sown during this sign produce good stalks and vines. Grapes are a good example.

TAURUS–*APRIL 21 TO MAY 21*

A fixed earth sign. Best time for sowing root-crop seed.

GEMINI–*MAY 22 TO JUNE 21*

A barren sign. Good time for sowing melon seed.

CANCER–*JUNE 22 TO JULY 22*

A cardinal water sign. The most productive time for any sowing and for transplanting.

LEO–*JULY 23 TO AUGUST 23*

A barren sign. Not a good time for sowing seed of any kind.

VIRGO–*AUGUST 24 TO SEPTEMBER 23*

A barren sign. Not a good time for sowing either, but good for flower blossom.

LIBRA–*SEPTEMBER 24 TO OCTOBER 23*

A cardinal air sign. The perfect time for sowing flower seed but bad for fruit.

SCORPIO–*OCTOBER 24 TO NOVEMBER 22*

A fixed water sign. The second-best sowing time, particularly for corn, pumpkins and squash.

SAGGITARIUS–*NOVEMBER 23 TO DECEMBER 21*

A masculine fire sign. An unfavorable time to sow or plant anything.

CAPRICORN–*DECEMBER 22 TO JANUARY 20*

A cardinal earth sign. A good all-round time to plant and sow those plants which produce an abundance of roots and branches.

AQUARIUS–*JANUARY 21 TO FEBRUARY 19*

A masculine air sign. Unfavorable generally for seed though excellent for laying out onions.

PISCES–*FEBRUARY 20 TO MARCH 20*

A cardinal water sign. Beneficial time for sowing anything. Plants which grow from seeds sown at this time are best adapted to withstand drought.

COMMITTING TO THE EARTH

"Therefore every gardener and owner ought to be careful and diligently to foresee, that the seeds committed to the earth be neither too old, dry, thin, withered, nor counterfeited, but rather ful, new and having juyce."
FROM *THE GARDENER'S LABYRINTH* BY THOMAS HILL BORN 1529

Sowing

PROTECTING NEWLY SOWN SEEDS FROM BIRDS

There is everything to be said for allowing the birds to have their share of newly planted seeds. However, if there is only a limited amount of seed for sowing, or where the seed is of a rare plant and every one being valuable, try this ancient anti-bird spray. Make an infusion of wheat or barley seed in wine (bring to the boil and allow to steep for ten minutes) and mix the strained solution with an ounce or two of Sneezewort (*Achillea ptarmica* – a medicinal herb). When it has cooled, water the area around the seed bed with the solution. The birds won't come near it.

"If seeds to be committed to the earth, are a little time before the bestowing, steeped in the juyce of Houseleeke or Singreen, they shall not onely be without harme preserved from Birds, Ants, field Mice and other spoilers of the garden."
FROM *THE GARDENER'S LABYRINTH* BY THOMAS HILL BORN 1529

ONE FOR THE BIRDS

To expect 100 per cent germination and fruition from sown seed is both unreasonable and unrealistic. The traditional ethic of both farmers and gardeners in former times was to sow generously to allow a percentage for the birds. This percentage, by rights, has always been one in four, but a better method requires more faith for it is a by-product of the ancient law of tithing. This requires the gardener to set aside a complete seed row – ten per cent of the crop – specifically for nature's need. It may seem a naive concept, but it has been common practice at many organic farms and gardens and with splendid results.

One for the rook, one for the crow,
One to die and one to grow.
Plant your seeds in a row,
One for pheasant, one for crow,
One to eat and one to grow.
TRADITIONAL RHYMES

MAKING SEED MOUSE-PROOF

Both mice and birds can play havoc in a garden where seed has been newly sown. Prevent this by moistening the seeds with paraffin before sowing.

BURYING BOTTLES IN SEED BEDS

To prevent cats, and most other animals, from damaging seed beds, bury several small bottles up to their necks in the soil where the seed has been sown. Fill the bottles with a few spoonfuls of any noxious-smelling liquid such as household ammonia. Cats will stay wide and clear.

THE ELBOW SOIL TEST

In the same way a parent tests the temperature of a baby's bath water with his or her elbow, so the sensitive seed sower tests the temperature of the soil before sowing. If the soil is too cold, seed will not germinate, but if the soil feels warm when your elbow is rested on it, then it will be warm enough for sowing.

GERMINATING SEEDS IN MANURE TEA

This method for encouraging seed to germinate faster and grow quickly produces wonderful results. It requires the making of "manure tea" in which a bucket containing half manure, half water is steeped for a day, strained and then diluted with more water until the brew is a light amber color. Soak the seeds in the brew overnight before planting.

STRATIFYING SEED

Some seeds will germinate more readily after a period of what some old gardeners called stratification – the practice of exposing the seed to frost. This is particularly effective with hardcoated seeds of many hardy plants and of numerous trees and shrubs. Place the seeds in shallow trays or boxes and cover them with a layer of sand. Place the trays outside in an exposed position during the winter months and then sow in the ordinary way during the spring. If frost is not forthcoming, seeds can be artificially stratified by placing them in the ice box in a refrigerator, or in the deep freeze. Remove and replace the seeds once or twice a week to reproduce natural frost conditions.

SOWING SMALL SEEDS

Some seeds, such as those from carrot and poppy, are very tiny. This makes sowing them a difficult process. To overcome the problem, place the seed in a sealed envelope with a small hole cut in one corner. The seed can then be sprinkled easily and accurately by gently tapping the envelope as required. Alternatively, mix the seed with a handful of fine sand and sprinkle along the drills in the normal way.

SOWING SEEDS WITH A CAKE-ICING BAG

To sow small seeds in an exact spot in a regular amount is extremely difficult. To overcome this problem, mix up a quantity of either flour or wallpaper paste to a good smooth consistency, then stir in the seeds. With the aid of an ordinary cake-icing dispenser, squeeze out the precise amount of paste in the exact spot.

ROLLING SEEDS IN AFTER SOWING

This custom is rarely observed these days and yet gardeners in former times swore by it as a means to help the germination of seeds. The method entails firming down the soil immediately after sowing using either the foot, the back of a spade, or a roller. A light covering of soil must then be sprinkled over the seed and the ground firmed again.

WATERING SEEDS WITH HOT WATER

Most newly sown seeds will germinate more readily if they are watered immediately after sowing with hot water from a fine rose sprinkler. After this initial watering, tepid water must be applied, never cold water straight from the tap. Germination and growth will be markedly improved than if cold water was used.

THE WATER TEST FOR SEEDS

This test to determine good seed from bad is not practical where really tiny seeds are concerned, but it's a good rule of thumb for beans, peas and other seed of similar size. Fill a tray or shallow pan with water and shake in the seed. Sound seeds will sink, leaving the less-than-perfect specimens floating on the surface.

STORING SEEDS IN SAND

Some seeds, notably the fleshy type from trees and shrubs, do not keep for any length of time in packets. In some cases the seeds can become so hard that germination can take anything from one to two years. To prevent this, and to keep the seeds in peak condition, store them in sand until required.

CREATING YOUR OWN SCENTED FLOWERS

This may seem an improbable feat of magic but try it and see –
it really does work. Buy a packet of your favorite annual-
flower seeds, but choose a variety which does not carry its
own fragrance. Soak the seeds overnight in scented water –
rose water is a good choice – and then dry them in the sun.
When the seeds have been planted and eventually grow, the
flowers will carry the scent of the original perfume.

Soon will the high Midsummer pomps come on,
Soon will the musk carnations break and swell,
Soon shall we have gold-dusted snap dragon,
Sweet William with his homely cottage smell,
And stock in fragrant blow.

FROM *THYRSIS* BY MATTHEW ARNOLD 1822–88

They say that when you plant a bean,
(A broad bean is the one they mean),
It should be dipped in paraffin.

If this surprising fact is true,
I wonder if the Creator knew;
And did he dip the Lily and the Rose
And every other scented flower that grows
In some sweet Heavenly dew,
Whose secret He, alone, The Great Creator, knew?

SCENT BY REGINALD ARKELL 1882–1959

SOWING BARLEY WHEN SLOE BLOSSOMS

To determine the correct time to sow barley, observe the wild sloe trees (blackthorn) and proceed with sowing when the sloe blossom is in its fullness.

CARROTS IN CAMPHOR

Before sowing carrot seed, crumble a handful of mothballs (camphor or naphthalene) and sprinkle over the soil, lightly working it in with a hoe. This will ensure protection against carrot fly.

POTATOES IN MOTHBALLS

When planting potato seed in the ground, place a mothball next to each tuber before covering with soil. This will stop slugs and other pests from eating the seed. Don't worry, the potatoes won't taste of mothballs!

Maundy Thursday is traditionally the best time for planting potato seed.

When you hear the cuckoo shout
'Tis time to plant your tatties out.
TRADITIONAL RHYME

TATTIES Old Scottish slang for potatoes.

SOWING SWEET PEAS ON ST PATRICK'S DAY

Sweet peas have always been planted traditionally on St Patrick's Day (March 17). It is said that the blooms of sweet peas planted on this day will be bigger and more fragrant than those planted before or after. The sticks used for supporting sweet peas must never be cut from an ash tree as this wood makes the plants recoil on touch.

Here are sweet peas, on tiptoe for a flight,
With wings of gentle flush, o'er delicate white.
JOHN KEATS 1795–1821

SOWING BEANS IN HAIR

Beans require a very rich and nutritious soil for a good bumper crop. To achieve this, plant them in a prepared trench to which a liberal quantity of hair has been added. Whether it comes as trimmings from your local hairdresser, or as horsehair from an old mattress, hair in general contains many valuable minerals and trace elements.

> *Plant kidney beans, if you be so willing,*
> *When elm leaves are big as a shilling.*
> *When elm leaves are as big as a penny,*
> *You must plant beans if you mean to have any.*

TRADITIONAL RHYME

THE SHILLING AND PENNY were part of the English currency before decimalization. A shilling measured approximately ⁷/₈ in. (22mm) in diameter, a penny measured 1¹/₄ in. (30mm).

SOWING BEANS IN NEWSPAPER

Runner beans are particularly thirsty plants and grow best when the soil in which they are sown remains cool and moist. One cheap and effective method of retaining water in the soil when growing beans is to place sheets of newspaper, along with manure and compost, in the bean trenches as they are dug. The newspaper will retain moisture for long periods, even in quite dry conditions.

SAVING SEED

Seeds sold in packets from seed merchants have become increasingly expensive in recent years. Our ancestors bought very little seed, for they saved their own each season and in this way perpetuated their own supplies year in and year out. It is a good habit to emulate and also very satisfying, and it will save you a lot of money!

As a general rule, seeds of all kinds should be stored in paper bags and kept in a dry, even temperature. It's wise to keep seeds out of the reach of rats and mice, and this can be achieved by suspending seed bags from the ceiling.

When harvesting, only use seed which has been allowed to fully ripen, particularly those which are formed in fleshy fruits such as tomatoes. However, make sure the fruit is ripe only, not rotten, otherwise poor germination will be likely.

Most vegetable seeds will keep for two years without losing vigor, but cabbages, radishes and turnips can be relied upon to germinate up to five years after harvesting. Cucumber and melon seed can be kept for ten years or more.

CHAPTER THREE

PLANTS AND PLANTING

Plant your taters (potatoes) when you will,
They won't come up before April.
TRADITIONAL RHYME

OLD-TIME GARDENERS *PLANTING*
—— *were a fund of*
tips and techniques. The simplicity of much of
their advice tends to obscure its ingenuity, based,
as it was, on **GENERATIONS OF EXPERIENCE.**

BOTTLES FOR LEEKS

Leeks are normally raised from seed in the open air during early spring, and the seedlings planted during early to mid-summer. Many an old gardener would make a small hole for each seedling with the neck of a wine or beer bottle.

FOIL FOR CABBAGES

When planting young cabbage seedlings, place a strip of aluminum foil around the rootstem. This will prevent cabbage-fly larvae attacking the plants.

PINE NEEDLES FOR STRAWBERRIES

To raise strawberry plants with fruit of the finest flavor, plant them in topsoil taken from around pine or spruce trees. Once established, mulch the strawberry plants with needles from these same trees. Your strawberries will never taste better.

NETTLES FOR BLACKCURRANTS

The best place to plant blackcurrants is in an old nettle bed, but if that's impractical, plant some nettles between the blackcurrants bushes. This will produce fruit of exceptional quality and keep the plants free of disease.

WATERS IMPROVED TREE PRUNER.

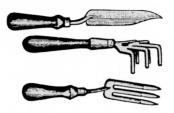

BRACKEN FOR FUCHSIAS

When planting fuchsias, dig a hole big enough to include a few bracken leaves around their roots. They will soon grow into strong vigorous plants with handsome blooms.

LAVENDER FOR CROCUSES

Birds love to pick crocus blooms and can cause much damage to the plants. However, plant crocus bulbs near lavender and birds won't touch them.

OLIVE STONES FOR GARLIC

Garlic will grow bigger and with a stronger flavor if you bruise the cloves a little before you plant them. Olive stones set around each plant will also stimulate its growth.

ROTATING HERBS

Old herbalists adhered religiously to certain rules when planting herbs. They would never plant the same herb, for example, in the same spot twice in succession, and they always replaced a "cool" herb with a "hot" one on a yearly rotation.

AFTERNOON PLANTING

The golden rule for setting out plants was always "after 4 p.m." and it is a practice well worth following. From this time of day the sun's heat is decreasing in intensity and plants will have the benefit of "settling in" during the coolest part of the day.

BANANAS AND MEAT FOR ROSES

Banana skins are a rich source of magnesium, sulphur, calcium, phosphates, silica and sodium – trace elements which plants need in order to grow healthier and which are often missing from soils. Laid just below the surface of the soil around rose trees and bushes, they will ensure a magnificent display of blooms.

Try lard or meat fat as yet another addition to the soil – roses love it! Plant a block of cooking lard or dripping beneath the roots of each new rose bush or tree. The results will be spectacular. Always plant parsley near roses to improve their fragrance.

Rose,
Unbent by winds, unchill'd by snows,
Far from the winters of the west,
By every breeze and season blest,
Returns the sweets by nature given
In softest incense back to Heaven....
LORD BYRON 1788–1824

GOOD COMPANIONS

The idea that plants interact with each other, either to their mutual benefit or harm, was common knowledge to gardeners even in the most ancient of times. Put into practice it can be of enormous help in the garden, encouraging healthy growth and fruition, and warding off pests and disease.

**PLANTS THAT HELP
EACH OTHER**

APPLES, CHIVES, NASTURTIUMS
TOMATOES, ASPARAGUS
CARROTS, BEANS
BEANS, CABBAGE
BEETROOT, ONIONS
STRAWBERRIES, BORAGE
CABBAGE, EARLY POTATOES
PEAS, CARAWAY
CARROTS, LEEKS
CAULIFLOWER, CELERY
CELERIAC, RUNNER BEANS
POTATOES, CHERRIES
RADISHES, CHERVIL
SWEET CORN, PEAS, CUCUMBERS
CABBAGE, DILL
GARLIC, ROSES
GOOSEBERRIES, TOMATOES
GRAPES, HYSSOP
LETTUCE, STRAWBERRIES
ONIONS, LETTUCE
PEAS, TURNIPS
ROSEMARY, CARROTS
SPINACH, STRAWBERRIES
SUNFLOWERS, CUCUMBERS
TOMATOES, PARSLEY
TURNIPS, PEAS.

**PLANTS THAT REPEL
EACH OTHER**

RUE, BASIL
RUNNER BEANS, POTATOES
BEETROOT, BEANS
CABBAGES, STRAWBERRIES
APPLES, CARROTS
CHERRIES, WHEAT
CUCUMBERS, POTATOES
FENNEL, TOMATOES
GARLIC, PEAS
GLADIOLI, BEANS
HYSSOP, RADISHES
PUMPKINS, POTATOES
RASPBERRIES, BLACKCURRANTS
SHALLOTS, PEAS
TOMATOES, GOOSEBERRIES.

GROWING ERICACEOUS PLANTS

How many a poor frustrated gardener will relate to the story below? Yet the fact remains that trying to grow ericaceous (acid-soil-loving) plants in ordinary garden soils is a wasted exercise. The lime in most soils will soon affect the plants and they will eventually succumb and die. The traditional answer to this problem is to provide a special peat bed where all the normal soil has been removed and replaced with peat, leaf mold and manure – an extremely expensive option. Another simpler and far less expensive way is to plant each rhodo-dendron, azalea, camellia etc. in a large flowerpot filled with the correct soil. Sink each pot in the garden so that its rim is just above ground. Situated like this, the plants will grow quite happily for years provided they are fed and watered.

I tried for twenty years or so,
To make my rhododendrons grow.
I sought new species, far and wide,
But still my rhododendrons died.

I danced around them, in a ring:
I watered them like anything,
And then I placed a bag of peat
Around my rhododendrons' feet.

Out of the peat, there came a lot,
Of lovely things I hadn't got:
Azaleas, Dahlias, London Pride,
An Iris and a Phyllis Bide –
But still my rhododendrons died.

STOWAWAYS BY REGINALD ARKELL 1882–1959

CHAPTER FOUR

CARE AND CULTIVATION

You've never finished working in a garden,
Until 'tis time for you to go to bed.
You're either squirting soapsuds on the roses,
Or picking all the pansies that are dead.
REGINALD ARKELL 1882–1959

The general — CARE AND *CULTIVATION*—
of plants requires the full attention of the gardener.
With BOTH EYES CONSTANTLY OPEN *for unwanted*
pests and diseases, and BOTH HANDS EMPLOYED *in*
the tasks of feeding, weeding, training and pruning,
it is A BUSY YET REWARDING TIME *in the garden.*

STOPPING LETTUCE BOLTING

If you leave mature lettuce in the ground for very long they will "bolt" (grow tall and flower prematurely) at which time they are inedible. If you have a row of mature lettuce which you simply cannot eat in time, retard their growth by giving them a shock to the system. Dig them up, leave them in the shade for an hour, then replant them. Such treatment forces the lettuce to adjust to the soil again before they can continue to grow, and that will take several days.

PRODUCING A BUMPER CROP OF RUNNER BEANS

Runner beans can be given a boost that is guaranteed to produce a truly bumper crop. When the leaves begin to turn limp and fall off, remove every leaf. Fill a bucket or two with manure, add water and stir thoroughly until it is liquid. Leave it for two to three days, then pour the liquid manure around the roots of the beans.

GROWING PERFECTLY STRAIGHT BEANS

Growing those extraordinarily straight, prize-winning runner beans is not left to luck. It can only be achieved by adopting an exceedingly tedious but effective method. Carefully tie lengths of cotton thread to the delicate tips of the immature beans. Tie a small weight to each thread so that the beans hang straight down. You will have to retie the thread every few days to prevent them being strangled.

GROWING RUNNER BEANS UP SUNFLOWERS

This truly charming way of growing runner beans makes attractive use of the sunflower's height and pole-like stem which is quite sturdy and strong enough to support climbing beans. The sunflowers must be sown as early as possible in the season to allow them to make a head start in growth over the beans. Come the allotted time to sow beans, the sunflowers will be a foot or two high, and by the time the beans have germinated and begun to climb upwards, the sunflowers will have reached a size and strength to support them. Sow two to three beans at the foot of each sunflower.

Eagle of flowers! I see thee stand,
And on the sun's noon-glory gaze:
With eye like his, thy lids expand
And fringe their disk with golden rays:
Though fix'd on earth, in darkness rooted there,
Light is thine element, thy dwelling air,
Thy prospect heaven.

FROM *THE SUNFLOWER* BY JAMES MONTGOMERY 1771–1854

GROWING PRIZE CABBAGES

Beer is a little-known plant food which has remarkable effects on the *Brassica* family. Cabbages respond particularly well to a regular dose of beer, but try it on all your vegetables and see how they grow.

GETTING THE RIGHT COLOR FOR TOMATOES

To assist the fruit to turn a good deep red, make a mixture of wood ash and burnt soil in equal proportions and apply it around the plants at the rate of two pounds per square yard.

GROWING VEGETABLES ON A TRELLIS

Excellent results can be achieved by growing certain vegetables and salads over a trellis. Both tomatoes and cucumbers respond splendidly to such a system of cultivation. By habit, the cucumber has a natural inclination to climb and its luxurious foliage looks quite wonderful when grown in this way. The same can be said for tomatoes, and the fruit produced will be superior in size, quantity and taste.

-Framework for training Cucumbers

PRODUCING UNBLEMISHED CARROTS

Use this method to ensure the shapely growth of unblemished carrots. After the carrot bed has been dug during the winter months, obtain a good quantity of sawdust from your local sawmill or timberyard and thoroughly soak it with paraffin. Evenly distribute the sodden sawdust over the prepared carrot bed and fork it into the soil. Repeat the procedure several days later only this time turn the soil slightly so that the bulk of the sawdust remains on the surface.

GROWING PERFECTLY SHAPED CUCUMBERS

Exhibition-standard cucumbers must be grown perfectly straight. To achieve this feat, obtain from a hardware store some lengths of clear plastic tubing about the diameter of the largest cucumber you can buy. Cut a tube to the length of a good-size cucumber and, at one end, drill or pierce two holes, one on each side of the tube. Thread some strong twine or string through the holes, and hang the tube beneath each cucumber. The cucumbers will grow into the tubes and remain straight, ready for picking.

GROWING NAMES ON FRUIT

This clever trick is sure to impress your friends, and it works equally well with apples, pears, plums or peaches. Cut out your initials (or any shape you wish) from paper; the size is determined by the fruit you are growing. Paste the cutouts on the side of the fruit exposed to the sun just before it begins to change color. When the fruit is ripe and ready for eating, remove the paper cutouts to reveal perfect copies.

PREVENTING CAMELLIA-BUD FALL

Bud fall-off from camellias, a not uncommon problem, is one that can ruin the appearance of these most beautiful of shrubs. To help prevent this, fork some of the soil away from about the roots, leaving just enough to hold the plants firmly in position. Loosen the soil beneath the roots and fill with coarse fibrous peat, loam and sand in equal proportions mixed together. Lightly prune the branches and remove one in five of the flower buds. This will sustain the buds that are left and will result in a fine display.

MAKING TEA ROSES SMELL STRONGER

There are many roses, both of the old-fashioned tea varieties and the modern hybrid teas, whose blossom has a fragrance, quite literally, of scented tea. To increase the strength and quality of this fragrance, make a habit of emptying the residue from your teapot (cold tea, leaves and bags) onto the soil around the roses. The flowers will produce a truly delicious perfume and the health of the roses will improve.

TEA LEAVES FOR CAMELLIAS

Tea leaves and cold tea (or tea bags) make a most beneficial mulch for camellias, rhododendrons and azaleas.

THE CUP THAT CHEERS BUT NOT INEBRIATES.

MAKING A YUCCA FLOWER

Yuccas are spectacular in bloom yet they are notorious for remaining flowerless for years on end. In the wild, the yucca is a desert plant and therefore most likely to flower when desert conditions are created. Dig a trench about eighteen inches wide all round the plant to reveal plenty of its roots. Cut away the roots completely, fill the trench with rocks and stones, then cover with just a shallow layer of soil. If this is done in early spring there is every chance the yucca will flower in the fall.

TURNING PINK HYDRANGEAS BLUE

Perform the conjuring trick of turning pink or white hydrangeas blue by burying a handful of rusty nails in the soil. Spread some nails on a shallow dish and spray them with water. Leave the dish outside, keeping the nails damp until they develop a healthy patina of rust, then plant them around the roots of the hydrangeas.

MAKING NAILS RUSTPROOF

Unless they are galvanized, nails for garden fencing and other construction work have only a limited life before they rust away. To make nails rustproof, mix together a pint of linseed oil with two ounces of black-lead (graphite) powder and stir thoroughly. Take the nails and heat them over an open fire until they are red hot. Dunk the nails in the mixture, drain away excess liquid and leave to dry.

SOOT FOR ONIONS

Onions will greatly benefit from a top-dressing of soot during their growing season. Ensure that no soot actually comes into contact with the onion bulbs or leaves.

WOOD ASH FOR LILIES

Lilies are flowers of great beauty and they require very personal attention if they are to produce their best blooms. A top dressing of wood ash will ensure a wonderful display.

BEER FOR FLOWERS

Ale is an excellent liquid food for flower beds and borders. Plants which grow very tall, such as hollyhocks, delphiniums and sunflowers, benefit from a weekly feed of beer.

MILK FOR HOUSEPLANTS

Make your own liquid houseplant food by rinsing empty milk containers with water. Use the slightly milky water like a proprietary liquid manure.

A SAUNA FOR CYCLAMEN

Cyclamen must always be watered from below, never by pouring water into the top of the flowerpots as this will rot the corms. They require moist conditions to stay healthy, and what really perks them up is a "sauna" in hot water every two weeks. At the required time of watering, pour boiling water into the bottom tray (see PEBBLES IN HOUSEPLANT TRAYS) and allow the steam to rise among the cyclamen foliage. Surprisingly this does no damage whatsoever to the roots but greatly benefits the plant in general.

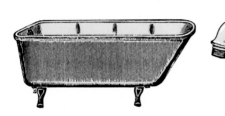

BATHS FOR HOUSEPLANTS

Indoor plants with strong fleshy leaves such as the India rubber plant (*Ficus elastica*), snake plant (*Sansevieria trifasciata Laurentii*), philodendron, and cheese plant (*Monstera deliciosa*) will greatly benefit from a regular "bath". It is virtually impossible to bathe large plants, but with normal-size plants in pots that can easily be handled, bathing plants is a straightforward procedure. Simply fill up a bath or sink with tepid water (body temperature) and add a little liquid soap. With one hand over the top of the flower pot to retain the soil, tip the plant upside down and totally submerge the foliage for a minute or two. This not only revives plants in warm weather but also helps to kill any insects such as whitefly that may happen to be lurking on the leaves.

PEBBLES IN HOUSEPLANT TRAYS

Many indoor plants require a moist environment in order to grow well and this is often difficult to create in dry warm interiors. Solve the problem by standing the flowerpots or containers in trays filled with small pebbles, just barely covered with water. This provides a perfect moist environment.

SOFT WATER FOR FEEDING PLANTS

Plants can be watered with ordinary drinking water, but they seem to do much better when they are given rainwater which has been softened. It is really easy to obtain perfectly soft water. Collect a quantity of rainwater in large shallow tubs, and expose it to the heat of the sun for two to three days.

Dissolve a little ordinary washing soda (sodium carbonate) in any water to increase its softness. Add about one ounce of washing soda to twelve gallons of water.

SODIUM CARBONATE   A white powdery compound used in the manufacture of detergents.

HOW TO SOFTEN WELL WATER

If the hardness of well or spring water is due to chalk or lime deposits it can be reduced simply by boiling. If it is due to more permanent mineral salts then soften it by adding a teaspoon of powdered quicklime to every ten gallons of water.

QUICKLIME (CALCIUM OXIDE) Exercise caution when handling quicklime. It is extremely caustic when mixed with water.

WATERING WITH WARM WATER

There is a belief that plants should never be watered with cold water as this gives them a shock to their system. Warm water works wonders with greenhouse crops such as cucumbers, peppers and tomatoes, and it can be used to encourage outside plants to grow faster and lusher.

CHAPTER FIVE

HARVESTING AND PRESERVING

The summer's horn indeed is full with crops;
And earlier toil its due reward has earned.
Now shall you reap and gather, store and stack
Your hay, your corn, your barley, your hops.
FROM THE LAND *BY VITA SACKVILLE-WEST 1892–1962*

IN THIS MODERN AGE *when we can buy fruit, vegetables and flowers from a supermarket at any time of year,* '*HARVEST TIME*' *has been rendered meaningless. It is to our loss that* THE NATURAL RHYTHM HAS BEEN BROKEN *– a rhythm to which our ancestors were finely attuned and in which they took great pride and pleasure, cannily prolonging the life of the crops they had* SAFELY GATHERED IN.

PROLONGING THE VEGETABLE HARVEST

During the growing season most gardens yield far more vegetables at any one time than can be consumed comfortably. There are ways, however, of curbing your harvest.

CAULIFLOWERS

If they begin to "hullow" (make premature small heads), lift the plants, lay them in (plant temporarily) beside a north-facing wall and thoroughly soak them with water. Planted like this, they will keep in good condition for up to three weeks. Another way is to bend several of the outer leaves inward over the hearts and tie them in place. This will prolong the hearts in excellent condition.

CABBAGES

Remove only the heart of the cabbage, leaving the lower leaves. This will provide a crop of young shoots in the fall which will be both tender and caterpillar-free.

CUCUMBERS

Cut cucumbers from the plant before they are fully developed and, either rest the stalk ends in an inch of water, or bury them in a box of dry sand.

PEAS AND BEANS

Gather the pods gradually and take only those that are well-filled. This will lengthen the productive life of the plants by at least fifty per cent.

TOMATOES

As soon as tomatoes begin to "color", gather some fruit and place in a dry dark cupboard to ripen slowly, leaving a percentage of the crop on the bush to ripen naturally for immediate use. To preserve stored tomatoes longer than normal, wrap each fruit in fresh nettle leaves. These leaves have properties which extend the life of the fruit and also promote the ripening of green tomatoes.

TURNIPS

Having lifted the roots, cut off the tops of those turnips that will not be consumed imminently. Store these roots in moist soil, where they will keep for weeks in good condition.

LONG-TERM STORAGE

As a general rule, harvest vegetables to be stored for winter in late summer or early fall. These vegetables should remain in perfect condition until the next season, but some vegetables fare best under certain specific conditions.

ARTICHOKES (CHINESE)
The tubers, which should normally be ready for eating in the fall, can be left in the ground throughout the winter. Individual tubers can be harvested as required, but they will discolor if exposed for any length of time before cooking.

ARTICHOKES (GLOBE)
The heads should be cut off, leaving them with long stalks that should be planted in moist sand in a frostproof shed or outbuilding. It is advisable to shorten the stalks by a fraction every week and replace them in the sand.

ARTICHOKES (JERUSALEM)
The tubers can be left in the ground until required or lifted in late fall or early winter and stored in bone-dry soil or sand in a cool shed or outbuilding.

BEETROOT
There are two ways of storing beet. The traditional way is to build a "clamp". Choose a dry corner in the garden, free from frost if possible, and away from overhanging trees. Dig a circular base six inches deep by approximately one yard in diameter. Fill the depression halfway with dry straw or ashes.

After removing the leaves with a sharp twist (do not use a knife) arrange the beet in circles with their crowns facing outwards. Cover them with sifted ashes and arrange another batch in similar fashion on top of the first but in a smaller circle. Continue until you have built a conical mound of beet, then cover it with four inches of straw. Overlay with four inches of sifted moist soil, but allow a tuft of straw to project from the top of the mound for ventilation.

The more straightforward method is to store beet in deep boxes of dry sand, ashes or sifted dry soil, in an upright position, crowns upwards. The boxes should be stored in a dry cool place to prevent sprouting and mold growth.

CABBAGES

Remove all the outer leaves and any that are discolored or damaged, then store cabbages in string bags or hammocks suspended from the roof of a cool dry room.

CARROTS

Maincrop carrots sown in late spring or early summer are the most suitable for storing. They should be lifted not later than midfall when their leaves have curled and lost their fresh green color. Remove the leaves as near to the crown as possible to prevent sprouting and store the carrots in a "clamp" outside or in boxes between two-inch layers of peat or sand.

CAULIFLOWERS

Cauliflowers can be left in the ground or stored in boxes of straw in a cool dry place.

CELERIAC

Celeriac can be left in the ground and lifted as required, or it can be stored in a "clamp" or in sand inside a cool dry shed. Remove all the leaves except for the central growth which must be left to prevent new leaves sprouting.

CELERY

Celery can be left in the ground until it is required for the table. In harsh weather, when heavy frosts are expected, heel the plants in with plenty of dry soil to protect them.

CHICORY

Store as for carrots.

FENNEL

Clumps of fennel can be lifted in the fall and replanted in fairly large boxes or pots of peat. They should be stored in a heated greenhouse or warm part of the house (50 to 60°F).

GARLIC

During midsummer, when the leaf tips turn yellow, garlic bulbs should be pulled from the soil. Allow them to ripen on the ground under the protection of glass (or polyethylene) for a week, then store them on some sort of a wire rack until all the foliage has withered. Finally, separate each bulb, remove soil and dirt, then string them together in a rope.

HORSERADISHES

Twist the tops off horseradishes and store them in sifted ashes or moist sand.

KOHLRABIES

Kohlrabies can be left in the ground throughout the winter.

LEEKS

Leeks can be left to survive in the ground over winter, but in severe conditions it is advisable to lift some for storage inside. Store them in boxes filled with sand, where they will keep for a month or more.

MARROW SQUASHES

Use only full-grown fruit and those which have full rounded butt ends. Cut one squash only from each plant. Store squashes in a kitchen or some other room where the temperature will not fall below 50°F. Lay them on sacking in boxes or on a shelf, but make sure the fruits are not in contact with each other. Alternatively, store them separately in string bags suspended from the ceiling.

ONIONS

Lift onions and allow them to ripen in a sunny place until the foliage has withered. The traditional method for storing onions is to form them into a rope which can then be hung in a dry, cool place. Alternatively, onions can be stored in shallow boxes or in string bags.

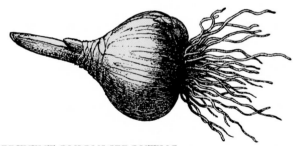

TO PREVENT ONIONS SPROUTING

To stop stored onions sprouting leaves, hold each rooted end over a flame for just a few seconds. The shock will not impair the onion's quality, but it will check any further growth.

> *Onion skins very thin,*
> *Mild winter coming in.*
> *Onion skins very tough,*
> *Coming winter very rough.*
> TRADITIONAL RHYME

POTATOES

It is essential to store only healthy unblemished tubers, and even these must be checked periodically for signs of disease. The simplest method is to spread out the tubers on straw or sacking in any airy shed or outbuilding and cover with the same. Exclude the light to prevent greening. Alternatively, potatoes can be placed carefully in sacks or boxes and kept in a larder, or store them outside in a straw- or bracken-filled "clamp" Keep a clamp dry by digging a trench around its base to drain water. Remove potatoes from a clamp during heavy frosts. New potatoes will keep till Christmas if they are buried in the garden inside a sealed tin as soon as they are harvested.

POTATO WATER FOR PATHWAYS

Light-colored stone paths eventually turn gray and grubby. Keep them clean by pouring over the stone the water in which potatoes have been cooked. Do this each time potatoes are on the menu.

SWEDES

Twist off swede tops, but leave a little of the greenery. Shorten the roots. Swedes can be stored in a "clamp", or in peat or sand in much the same way as carrots.

SALSIFIES

In dry districts, salsify roots can be left in the ground. In high-rainfall areas, lift the roots and store them in dry sand.

SHALLOTS

Once the foliage has turned yellow in midsummer lift shallot bulbs and allow them to dry in a sunny place. Store them in shallow trays or in bundles where sufficient ventilation will keep them cool and dry.

TOMATOES

Green tomatoes can be wrapped in tissue paper, newspaper or flannel and kept in the dark until ripe.

TURNIPS

Store as for swedes.

STORING FRUIT

As with vegetables, only sound, unblemished and disease-free fruit can be stored successfully. Never remove stalks as this encourages decay. And don't pick fruit that's still wet with rain or dew if you plan to store it.

APPLES

Pick apples just before they are perfectly ripe and before the frosts set in. Take care not to include any "falling apples", which may be infested with maggots. Gather the apples in the afternoon and lay them out very carefully in heaps inside a cool dry storage space to "heat" for two weeks. Wrap each apple individually in tissue paper and store in shallow trays, boxes or on shelves – in single layers with none of them touching. A cool, dark but well-ventilated cellar is ideal, but a shed or similar place will do. The floor of the storeroom should be sprinkled with water from time to time to keep the air moist and stop the fruit shriveling. Periodically inspect the fruit and dispose of any diseased or decaying specimens.

Til St Swithin's Day (July 15) be past,
the apples be not fit enough to taste.
TRADITIONAL SAYING

PEARS

Only the late-fruiting varieties are suitable for storing. Store in the same way as apples.

A pear year, a dear year;
a cherry year, a merry year;
a plum year, a dumb year.
TRADITIONAL SAYING

MAKING CUT FLOWERS LAST LONGER

As a general rule adding a pinch of salt to water in a vase will increase the life of cut flowers. To increase their fragrance, lay them in a basin of water for an hour directly after cutting.

All flowers cut in sunshine should be left to stand in water in the shade before being placed in a vase. Individual flower varieties should be treated as follows:

FLOWERS WITH HARD STEMS
Roses, honeysuckle, lilac and other flowers with hard stems will keep longer if the stems are split and the bark peeled from their ends. Cut off a small portion of the stem every day and change the water frequently.

CHRYSANTHEMUMS
Char the ends of chrysanthemum stems over a gas or candle flame immediately after the flowers have been cut and then put them in water.

ASTERS
Before you place asters in a vase, soak their stems in a quart of water plus a teaspoon of sugar for two hours.

AZALEAS
Burn the ends of azalea stems before placing them in water.

CAMELLIAS
Allow camellias to stand in slightly salty water for an hour before transferring them to fresh water in a vase.

CHERRY BLOSSOM
Don't cut cherry blossom. Break the stems and dip them in boiling water, then arrange the blossom in cold water.

Here in this sequestered close,
Bloom the hyacinth and rose;
Here beside the modest stock,
Flaunts the flaming hollyhock;
Here without a pang, one sees,
Ranks, conditions and degrees.
FROM *A GARDEN SONG* BY AUSTIN DOBSON 1840–1921

DAFFODILS

Stand daffodils in an inch of cold water and store them in a refrigerator for a couple of hours. Don't over water daffodils – too much will harm them – and never arrange them together with other cut flowers as their stems excrete poisons which are detrimental to anything standing with them in a vase of water.

Daffodowndilly has come to town,
In a yellow petticoat and a green gown.
TRADITIONAL RHYME

DAHLIAS

The lower part of dahlia stems should be stripped bare and placed immediately in hand-hot water (as hot as your hand will bear). Having soaked them for a while, place the flowers in darkness for several hours before displaying them.

DELPHINIUMS

Treat them like asters.

FORGET-ME-NOTS (MYOSOTIS)

Dip forget-me-not stems in boiling water for a few seconds before placing them in cold water.

FREESIAS

Add several drops of any alcohol to a pint of water. Stand freesias in this solution for three hours before you arrange them in fresh water.

GENTIANS

Crush the ends or burn the tips of gentian stems before totally submerging both flowers and stems in water for two hours.

To create a little flower is the labour of ages.
WILLIAM BLAKE 1757–1827

GARDENIAS

Put gardenias in a cardboard box and spray them thoroughly with water. Place the box in a refrigerator for about two hours before placing the flowers in a vase.

GLADIOLI

Gladioli should be gathered in the late afternoon. Choose flower heads with one or two open blooms only on the stem. They should be left in the sun for twenty minutes to "soften" which will ensure long-lasting flowering in water.

HYDRANGEAS

Crush hydrangea stems and stand them in a saucepan containing vinegar until it changes color, then arrange them in cold water in the vase.

IRISES

Soak iris stems in boiling water for three minutes, then stand them in iced water for two hours.

LILIES

Holding the flowers upside down, let cold water from a tap flow over them for about a minute before placing lily stems in deep water.

If lilies be plentiful, bread will be cheap.
TRADITIONAL SAYING

LILIES OF THE VALLEY (CONVALLARIA)

Stand lily-of-the-valley stems in boiling water for two minutes before placing them in cold water for two hours. Transfer the flowers to a vase.

NARCISSI

Carefully squeeze out the juicy sap from narcissi stems and place them in cold water for one hour. Turn the flowers upside down under a tap and allow cold water to flow over them for several minutes before standing them in a vase.

PEONIES

Gather peonies just before the flowers open and put them in cold water immediately.

POPPIES

Pick poppies a few hours before they open, preferably in the late evening for the following day's display. Char the ends of their stems over a flame before standing them in a vase.

> *Pleasures are like poppies spread,*
> *You seize the flow'r, its bloom is shed.*
> ROBERT BURNS 1759–96

ROSES

Stand rose stems in boiling water for three minutes, then place them in a vase of cold water to which a pinch of salt has been added.

> *Yet the rose has one powerful virtue to boast,*
> *Above all the flowers of the field,*
> *When its leaves are all dead and fine colours are lost,*
> *Still how sweet a perfume it will yield.*
> ISAAC WATTS 1674–1748

SWEET PEAS (LATHYRUS ODORATUS)

Try to pick sweet peas early enough to catch the dew still on them. This will ensure their color lasts longer than if they were gathered in full sunshine.

TULIPS

Stand tulips in boiling water for one minute before placing them in a vase.

VIOLETS

Place violets upside down in water for a few minutes.

> *If violets bloom at autumn time,*
> *Whose soil they grow on will surely die.*
> TRADITIONAL SAYING

PRESERVING FLOWERS WHOLE

Complete plants, flowers and even small branches in bloom can be preserved in their entirety using this method. Procure an earthenware pot or jar, large enough for the plant to be accommodated without any part of it touching the sides. Stand the plant in the center of the pot and very carefully trickle in perfectly dry silver sand until the whole plant is covered. Place the full pot in a warm oven for two to three hours. The plant can then be kept in the pot for months in perfect condition until it is required for display.

> *See how the flowers, as at parade,*
> *Under their colours stand displayed:*
> *Each regiment in order grows,*
> *That of tulip, pink and rose.*
> FROM *THE GARDEN* BY ANDREW MARVELL 1621–78

REVIVING LIMP FLOWERS

Sometimes, cut flowers will droop in hot weather, or if they have to travel any distance without water. The best "pick-me-up" for limp flowers is aspirin. First place the flowers in boiling water and leave them in a cool dark place until the water has cooled. Cut off the ends of their stems and place them in fresh water plus two aspirin tablets.

CHAPTER SIX

PESTS AND PESTILENCE

As I sat under a poplar tall,
I saw nine pests come over the wall.
I saw nine pests come wandering by:
A slug, a snail and a carrot fly...
REGINALD ARKELL 1882–1959

To hear some people talk of their garden you would think they were referring more to a BATTLEGROUND *than to a place of peace and tranquility. They speak of the* "WAR AGAINST SLUGS" *or* "FIGHTING BACK *the weeds",, and if one* *PEST* *is prevalent they say their garden* "is UNDER ATTACK" *or* "has been taken over" *by so and so. This, sadly, is the modern attitude and the solution is to reach for the chemical spray. Those wise gardeners of yesteryear boxed clever with pests, often outwitting them. But if they became a nuisance, there were ingenious and simple methods to* SOLVE A PROBLEM.

SLUGS AND SNAILS

An abundance of slugs and snails can decimate a vegetable plot overnight so clever precautions are essential. Choose from among these varyingly effective methods of control:

"As soon as the snails appear upon any part of the trees, endeavour as much as possible to destroy them; and the only method is this:

First pull off all the worst leaves that are infested with them; that is, such as are shrivelled, or much curled up; then strew some tobacco dust over all the branches and leaves; let this remain on the trees two or three days, then you may wash it off."

FROM *EVERY MAN HIS OWN GARDENER* BY THOMAS MAWE 1767

NO-LEGGED PESTS

WORMS

Worms are generally of immense value in the garden where they break down decomposable matter into fine humus and aerate the soil. However, they can render a fine lawn un-sightly when they cover the turf with wormcasts. Fill a coarse canvas bag or sack with two pounds of either horticultural lime or mustard and place it in a bucket or tub of water. Drain off the lime or mustard water and sprinkle it over the lawn. This will soon bring the worms to the surface.

Another effective method for raising worms is to take ten ripe horse chestnuts and boil them for an hour in a quart of water. Leave it to cool, then drain off the water and spray it over the soil. These methods of eradication do *not* kill worms, but merely bring them to the surface where they can be collected and transported elsewhere.

Discourage worms by digging wood ash into the soil before laying a lawn.

Barriers

Slugs and snails hate rough, sharp surfaces. Lay a six-inch wide trail of sharp sand, egg shells, chalk or fine grit around the area to be protected. Alternatively, surround the young plants with roofing slates or some similar thin flat material and cover them with a paste made up of thick oil and soot.

Aversions

Soot, wood ash and salt are sufficiently noxious to keep slugs and snails at bay. Liberally sprinkle one or more of these substances over the ground just before nightfall.

Foils

Slugs and snails can be enticed away from plants you wish to protect by offering them a more appealing meal. Create a "slug salad" from tender young lettuce, bean shoots and so on, and place it in a heap on the soil near to the plants. The next morning, the congregation can be removed elsewhere.

Another effective remedy is to sink a half-full jar of beer in the ground close to the threatened plants. At night, slugs and snails will come out to drink the beer, fall in and drown.

Alternatively, pick a few large rhubarb leaves in the evening and place them upside down among the plants. At dawn the slugs and snails will seek shelter under the leaves where they will lie waiting to be found and disposed of. If there's no rhubarb, use any other large-leafed plant or straw.

Plant deterrents

Slugs and snails dislike certain aromatic plants, and they avoid areas of the garden where they are growing. The common sage (*Salvia officinalis*) is particularly effective, as is the scarlet sage (*Salvia splendens*). Try also thyme (*Thymus*) and hyssop (*Hyssopus officinalis*).

When snails climb up the stalks of grass, wet weather is at hand.
TRADITIONAL SAYING

DISCOURAGING BIRDS

Birds can be both beneficial and an outright nuisance in the garden; beneficial because they eat harmful insects, slugs and snails, a nuisance because of their liking for newly-sown seed and certain tender young plants. To scare them off, try one or more of the following tricks:

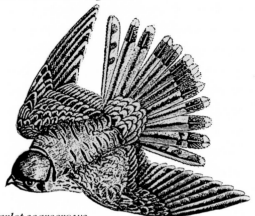

Scarlet scarecrows

The good old-fashioned, traditional scarecrow will have a lot more clout in its effectiveness if it is dressed in predominently red clothing. Research has proved that red is the most off-putting color for birds and they are least likely to approach anything of size in this color stood in the garden.

Black cotton in fruit trees and bushes

This very old standby is particularly effective in fruit trees and bushes where birds can inflict severe damage to both bud, blossom and young fruit. Build a web by tying strong black thread between all the branches. Birds have difficulty in judging the distance between the threads and will shy away rather than risk becoming entangled.

Feathered potatoes

One or two potatoes into which feathers have been inserted are good bird scarers. Hang the potatoes from string tied to sticks and place these in the seed bed or among young plants.

Glass wind chimes

Wind chimes are particularly effective among soft fruit bushes. Tie some small pieces of glass onto lengths of strong twine in such a way that they collide when suspended freely. Hang several chimes among the bushes so that at the slightest breeze the glass tinkles – very offputting to birds.

DISCOURAGING CATS

Two things to avoid having in a garden if you really want to discourage cats are a bird feeder, for obvious reasons, and the aromatic herb catmint (*Nepeta*) which cats adore. To rid the garden of cats try this ingenious method:

The false snake
Cut up an old hose-pipe into two-foot lengths and place them around the garden. Trespassing cats that are causing a nuisance will assume the tubes are snakes and keep well away.

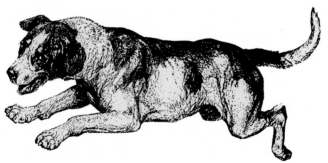

DISCOURAGING DOGS

The one plant that dogs detest is the common rue (*Ruta graveolens*). Plant several of these near to a gate or other entrance to the garden as a deterrent to any dog.

DISCOURAGING MOLES

Delightful as moles are, and one should never kill them, they can be a nuisance in a garden. Their tunneling disturbs the roots of plants which inevitably damages growth and may even kill them, and on a fine lawn moles can be nothing short of disastrous. If moles prove to be a problem then positive action is called for:

Digging out moles
Sit in a secluded area of the garden with a good vantage point of the mole hills. Sooner or later you will see a fresh hill appear. Take a spade and approach very quietly. Put the spade into the soil behind the hill, quickly push down and turn out the hill and earth beneath – mole will be there. The humane way to dispatch him is to take him out into the country, miles away from your plot, to continue his work elsewhere.

Wind in the bottle
A method which works well, although a little unconventional, is to sink into the ground among the mole hills several empty wine bottles, necks uppermost. The bottles should have just a couple of inches of neck showing above soil level. When the wind blows, the bottles will produce a singing sound which moles cannot stand. They will very soon remove themselves from the plot.

Plant deterrents
One old-time method for discouraging moles was to plant plenty of caper spurge (*Euphorbia lathyrus*) or milk spurge (*Euphorbia lactea*) in the garden. Apparently, moles hate the smell of these plants.

Mothballs
The smell of mothballs (camphor or naphthalene) is loathsome to moles. Place several balls in the mole tunnels and the creatures will soon disappear.

DISCOURAGING MICE

A barrier of prickly leaves

Place some leaves of gorse, holly or some other prickly-leaved plant among seed beds or plants that are under threat from hungry mice. They will soon deter any mouse foolish enough to approach.

Cat bathwater

A simple, ingenious and, apparently, effective method for dispelling mice is to wash a cat and sprinkle the water over the soil or plants to be protected. Mice will smell the cat and keep well away.

Plant deterrents

Mice do not like the smell of elder leaves (*Sambucus nigra*), milk spurge (*Euphorbia lactea*), spearmint (*Mentha spicata*), chamomile (*Chamaemelum nobile* and *Matricaria chamomilla*) and oleander (*Nerium oleander*). Plant one or more of these plants in the vegetable plot to keep mice at bay.

DISCOURAGING RATS

Tar-covered rags

Rats have such an aversion to tar that the merest whiff of it will send them scurrying. Cut some old rags into thickish strips and thoroughly soak them in a proprietary tar oil. Scatter these strips among vegetables or the seed bed for a perfectly rat-free garden.

Plant deterrents

Rats do not appreciate the smell of valerian (*Valeriana officinalis*) crown imperial (*Fritillaria imperialis*), the milk spurge (*Euphorbia lactea*), and the sea onion (*Scilla maritima*). Grow them wherever rats are a nuisance.

DISCOURAGING RABBITS

Fox oil

A substance called fox oil is invaluable in protecting vegetable foliage from the ravages of wild rabbits. It is a brown oily liquid sometimes known as oil of man, stink oil or animal oil (*Oleum animalis*), hartshorn or bone oil. A pharmacy is the most likely source for fox oil.

Make up a mild solution of soft soap and water, and add to it enough fox oil to turn the solution the color of weak coffee. Stir briskly. This solution will not harm even the most tender of foliage, particularly if it is sprayed onto the plant, but fox oil is poisonous so do not spray foliage which is for eating. To protect edible crops, soak some lengths of stout string in pure fox oil and peg them out around the vegetable plot at a height of about six inches.

FOX OIL. An organic chemical preparation, dark brown in color with a pungent odor. Contains pyridine and hydrocarbons, obtained by the destructive distillation of bones.

Plant deterrents

Rabbits are very sensitive to certain plants and will avoid any ground where they are growing. A liberal planting of foxgloves (*Digitalis*) around the vegetable garden will guarantee a rabbit-free area. Rabbits also have an aversion to onions, and any vegetable plot with a good sowing of onions will be safe from these pests.

Flowers are also at risk. Rabbits can cause havoc among the young shoots of many perennials. As a back-up precaution to the methods already described, plant several dill plants (*Anethum graveolens*) in flower beds and borders. Rabbits simply adore this plant and if any break through your first line of defense they will make a beeline for the dill, all other plants being forgotten in their enthusiasm for their favorite food.

DISCOURAGING PESTS WITH DUNG

You may have noticed that grey squirrels, which are increasing in number in urban areas, take a delight in raiding gardens to feed on succulent springtime tulip, hyacinth and crocus bulbs. As squirrels are afraid of cats, the remedy is simple: sprinkle the contents of a cat-litter tray in the area where you have planted bulbs.

If it is the cats themselves that are proving to be a nuisance, make friends with the lion tamer the next time a circus comes to town and scrounge a bucket or two of lion dung to spread on the garden. Even though domestic cats are unlikely to have encountered a lion, the smell of the dung will give them the impression that somewhere in the vicinity a large ferocious beast is lurking that they should avoid at all costs.

SAVING GNAWED TREES

When the bark of a tree has been gnawed by rabbits, squirrels or other animals, take action to prevent the tree from disease and possibly death. Trim the bark in the immediate vicinity of the wound and ensure the damaged area is cleansed thoroughly. Trim a strip of bark from a newly felled tree. This strip should be slightly wider than the exposed area of the wound. Place it over the wound with its top and bottom edges tucked under the existing bark. Finally, tie the strips in place and pour grafting wax over the whole area.

DISCOURAGING ANTS

Ants, on the whole, are useful, harmless creatures, but serious infestations can be bothersome and unpleasant. Discourage them as follows:

Plant deterrents
If ants habitually invade your fruit trees, take some lupin blooms, crush them and rub the juice around the bottom of the tree trunks early in the year. This will stop ants climbing the bark.

Ants dislike lavender (*Lavendula*), pot marigold (*Calendula officinalis*), African marigold (*Tagetes erecta*), tansy (*Tanacetum vulgare*), pennyroyal (*Mentha pulegium*) and chives (*Allium schoenoprasum*), so plant some in your garden to keep these insects at bay.

Baking yeast
Ordinary baking yeast is quite lethal to ants. Mix it with a sugar solution and spread it on pieces of bark placed around the roots of trees or other areas to be protected.

Camphor
A teaspoon of camphor on or around an ants' nest will quickly disperse the colony. Naphthalene and paraffin are equally effective.

Chalk and pepper
For some reason ants hate moving over chalk or pepper. Spread a liberal amount of either around threatened plants and use cayenne pepper if possible.

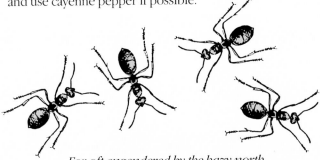

For oft engendered by the hazy north,
Myriads on myriads, insect armies warp,
Keen in the poisoned breeze; and wasteful eat,
Through buds and bark, in the blackened core
Their eager way.
JAMES THOMPSON 1700–48

DISCOURAGING APHIDS

The array of insects collectively known as aphids include three which perhaps cause the most damage in the garden – greenfly, blackfly and woolly aphis. To prevent their colonization use one or more of the following methods:

Nettle manure
Harvest a crop of stinging nettles (*Urtica dioica*) and steep a bunch in a bucket of water for five days. Dilute one part of this "nettle manure" with five parts of water and spray it onto plants to ward off aphids.

Garlic
Plant one or two garlic cloves among rose bushes and they will remain aphid-free. Likewise, an infusion of garlic crushed into water and sprayed over affected plants will soon dispel these pests.

Rhubarb soap
Take two pounds of rhubarb leaves and shred them into two pints of water. Boil them for half an hour and strain off the liquid. Take two ounces of liquid soap and one pint of water, and mix this with the rhubarb solution. Spray it onto healthy plants regularly to prevent infestation, and onto affected plants to eradicate the aphids.

Plant deterrents
Nasturtiums planted around the base of apple trees will prevent woolly aphides from infesting the trees. Likewise hyssop, lavender, sage, thyme, dill and birch trees all have adverse affects on aphids and are worth planting in or near the vicinity of vulnerable plants. Chervil (*Anthriscus cerefolium*) is a very effective deterrent for aphids which infest lettuce. Plant them between rows.

Many mayflies proclaim a warm summer.
TRADITIONAL SAYING

DISCOURAGING CATERPILLARS

Butterflies are beautiful insects, but the offspring of certain species are not so welcome, particularly among cabbages growing in the vegetable plot. Discourage them using one of the following methods:

Grass mowings
A thin coating of newly mown grass cuttings spread around cabbages, broccoli and similar plants will keep them caterpillar-free. No one knows why this works but work it does.

Sour milk
Make a solution of sour milk and a little lemon juice or vinegar. Spoon this into the center of each cabbage once a week for an effective deterrent.

Plant deterrents
Grow either wormwood (*Artemesia absinthium*) or southernwood (*Artemesia abrotanum*) among cabbages or around the perimeter of the patch. Their pungent aroma will discourage any curious butterfly or wandering caterpillar.

The caterpillar on the leaf,
Repeats to thee thy mother's grief,
Kill not the moth nor butterfly,
For the last judgement draweth nigh.
WILLIAM BLAKE 1757–1827

DISCOURAGING EARWIGS

Earwigs are not normally considered to be pests, but too many of them among dahlias and soft-fruit bushes and trees can be tiresome.

Paper or plant-tube traps
This method is excellent for catching and disposing of earwigs among wall-grown nectarines and peaches. Obtain the hollow stems of elder or sunflowers, or alternatively, make some tubes from rolled paper. Suspend these traps among the branches at night and, each morning, blow the insects out of the tubes where they have been hiding into a bottle filled with water.

Plant-pot traps
Fill some six-inch flowerpots with woodshavings or straw and support them upside down over garden canes or sticks. Earwigs will crawl up into the pots and can be disposed of each morning.

DISCOURAGING FLEAS

Plant deterrents
Certain plants have a detrimental effect on fleas. These include bog myrtle or sweet gale (*Myrica gale*), chamomile (*Anthemis nobilis*), hollyhock (*Althaea*) and pyrethrum (*Chrysanthemum coccineum*) – an extremely useful plant from which it is possible to obtain an extract that is a very effective general insecticide. It is available commercially. Ferns are also said to ward off fleas.

"If, when you first hear the cuckoo, you mark well where your right foot standeth, and take up that earth, the fleas will by no means breed where any of that same earth is scattered."

THOMAS HILL BORN 1529

DISCOURAGING FLIES

Flies are useful insects in as much as they provide a prime food-source for birds. But flies such as the apple sawfly, cabbage-root fly, carrot fly and celery fly are lethal intruders. However, don't use insecticides to eradicate these pests because chemicals may poison the birds. Use one of the age-old methods instead.

Flypaper gum strips
Hang common-or-garden flypaper strips among apple trees to prevent apple sawflies making their home there.

Tarred-felt barrier
Obtain some tarred roofing felt. Cut out four-inch squares and, in the center of each one, punch a $^3/_8$ inch hole. When planting seedling cabbages or cauliflowers, push their roots through a square. This is a most effective measure against cabbage-root fly.

Paraffin and creosote trails
The carrot fly depends almost entirely on its sense of smell to home in on carrot crops. Lay between the rows of vegetables trails of sawdust or woodshavings soaked in paraffin or creosote to put the carrot flies off the scent.

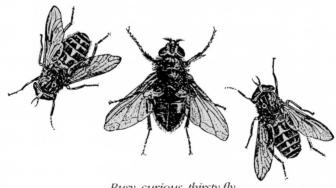

Busy, curious, thirsty fly,
Drink with me, and drink as I;
Freely welcome to my cup,
Coulds't thou sip, and sip it up.
Make the most of life you may;
Life is short, and wears away.
WILLIAM OLDYS 1696–1761

Home-made spray

Prevent an outbreak of onion fly or turnip sawfly by spraying either plant with a mixture of four fluid ounces of paraffin, four ounces of liquid soap and two gallons of water.

Spray soot mixed with water over celery to prevent infestation by the celery fly.

A dressing of soot on lawns during the spring will check the outbreak of the destructive grubs that eventually grow into crane flies or "daddy longlegs".

Plant deterrents

Both the African marigold (*Tagetes erecta*) and French marigold (*Tagetes patula*) will ward off flies, but most effective is southernwood (*Artemesia abrotanum*) whose pungent-smelling leaves keep most insects at bay. Two other plants that flies detest are tansy (*Tanacetum vulgare*) and stinging nettles (*Urtica dioica*). Both are wild flowers that can be allowed to flourish in a corner of a garden.

Use a spray made from an infusion of wormwood (*Artemesia absinthium*) to treat fly-infested plants.

Flies do not infest walnut trees, so plant one in the garden to keep it healthy and to provide a plentiful supply of leaves to bring indoors and keep the home free from flies.

DISCOURAGING MOTHS

Most of the strong aromatic herbs can be employed to discourage moths. Try wormwood, southernwood, rosemary, sage, santolina, lavender and marjoram.

Lavender bags

Balls of cotton wool soaked in lavender oil, or dried lavender flowers tied up in a muslin bag, can be suspended from sticks distributed among plants to ward off marauding moths.

DISCOURAGING WASPS

Wasps hate the smell of ammonia yet are addicted to sweet substances. These two facts form the foundation of protective measures against these largely harmless creatures. Unfortunately, wasps also happen to adore sweet, ripening fruit and so measures must be taken to keep them at bay:

Ammonia repellent
Mix equal amounts of water and ammonia, and fill several glass jars with the liquid. Suspend the jars from twine or wire among the branches of fruit trees.

Sugar-water traps
If wasps become real pests then set traps to catch them. Hang several jars filled with sugared water or beer in the branches of fruit trees. The wasps will be unable to resist the sweet liquids, fall in and drown.

Nylon-stocking barrier
An innovative way of protecting almost-ripe grapes, is to draw over each bunch a woman's nylon stocking. This will foil even the most determined wasp.

RELIEF FROM WASP STINGS

Always grow the herb summer savory (*Satureja hortensis*) in the garden, for a sprig of its leaves rubbed over a wasp's sting will bring speedy relief.

CURES FOR INSECT BITES & STINGS
The majority of poison contained in insect bites and stings is of an acid nature and common sense points to the use of an alkali for a cure. The most easily obtainable alkaline substances are the following, and all are highly recommended for external application – remove the sting first of course: – Ammonia, soap, washing soda, onion juice, tobacco water, wood ashes, dock leaves, tomato leaves and potato leaves.

SOME ALL-PURPOSE INSECTICIDES

Laurel leaves
Several bruised or pulped laurel leaves (*Prunus lauroc-erasus*) left in a bowl overnight in a greenhouse or cold frame make a most effective fumigant. The leaves give off a substance called glucoside when fermenting which is deadly to most insects.

Garlic soap
Fresh cloves of garlic crushed into a liquid-soap solution is invaluable as a spray against many insect pests in the garden. Insects loathe the smell of garlic and cannot cope with the stickiness left by the soap.

Salt solution or brine
Seawater or a strong salt solution can be an effective insect deterrent, though spraying several times a week will be necessary for it to work well.

Dead-insect solution
This rather revolting method has had a long history in gardening circles. Collect as many dead slugs, snails, worms and insects as will fill a jar, and cover them with water. Allow them to decompose, which eventually produces the most foul-smelling concoction imaginable. Dilute this solution with ten parts water and use as an insecticide.

Rhubarb
An infusion of rhubarb leaves in water makes a cheap and useful insecticide. Use three pounds of leaves in six pints of water. This mixture is poisonous and should be labeled accordingly. Add liquid soap to increase its effectiveness.

Flour
Insects hate landing on leaves heavily dusted with flour – obviously of no use in wet weather.

Green potatoes
When exposed to light, potatoes eventually turn green and become poisonous. Boil one pound of green potatoes in a pan of water, strain off the liquid and, when cool, use it as an effective insect killer and repellent.

PESTILENCE

Fungi, molds, blights, scabs, rots, spots, rusts, mildews and damping off are pestilences which occur in the garden. Their variety is enormous and space allows only a list of general preventatives and cures, plus one or two specific methods for the most common plant ailments. The prime prevention against most of these maladies, however, is good feeding and cultivation in the right conditions.

Onion juice
Place a large bunch of onion leaves (not the bulb) in a bucket of water and allow them to soak for four days. Spray the strained liquid liberally over plants once every two weeks from early spring onwards to prevent mildew, or every few days for infected plants.

Nasturtiums
The cheerful annual climbing or dwarf nasturtiums grown round the base of fruit trees or among soft fruit bushes will help prevent most attacks of mildew. Try treating infected plants with a spray made from an infusion of nasturtium flowers and leaves.

Methylated alcohol
A spray of methylated alcohol is a good all-round cure for mildew on brassica crops.

Horsetail, bracken and elder
The common flowerless horsetail (*Equisetum arvense*) infused in water makes an excellent spray for mildew and blackspot on roses. Put an ounce of dried horsetail in two pints of water and boil for half an hour. Dilute the solution with four parts water and stir well before spraying. Both the common bracken (*Pteridium aquilinum*) and elder (*Sambucus nigra*) have leaves which can be used in the same way.

Those that would grow this useful root,
Free from blight and maggots,
Must freely use both lime and soot,
And they will have fine carrots.

WILLIAM GAIN 1956

AVOIDING CLUB ROOT

Brassicas and some allied plants are prone to club root which is a debilitating disease. Immunity from attack can be obtained by "puddling" the roots before planting. Take several plants in the hand and brush the roots to and fro in a mixture of equal parts of horticultural lime, clay and soot before settling them in the soil. The mixture should be the consistency of cream and should cover the roots completely.

MOTH BALLS IN PEACH TREES

Hang several bunches of moth balls in a peach tree just before the leaves bud to prevent unsightly peach-leaf curl in the spring.

One year's seed is seven year's weed.
TRADITIONAL RHYME

TOMATOES AND BLIGHT

A dead tomato plant suspended in an apple tree over winter will keep it free from blight. Alternatively, a tomato plant can be burnt beneath the tree; the smoke rising up through the branches acts as an effective fumigant.

WEEDS

Weeds are mostly wild flowers growing in the wrong place, but there are a handful of persistent invaders that really are nothing but weeds. Hoeing and mulching is normally sufficient to keep down weeds, but for a real invasion, try one of these deterrents:

Clearing weeds from pathways
Choose a period when you think it is unlikely to rain for several days, then scatter dry salt on overgrown pathways until a white film is discernible and leave it without watering until the weeds are destroyed. Alternatively, sprinkle a boiling-hot salt solution over the weeds, or a solution of one pint of creosote to one gallon of water. For gravel paths, water mixed with salt, ashes and tobacco will kill weeds most effectively.

Ridding the garden of couch grass (*Agropyron repens*)
Badly overgrown areas of couch grass can be cleared by sowing the ground in which it grows with turnip seed. The turnips will gradually cause the couch to wither and die. Another good method is to sow either lupins or tomatoes, both of which have a detrimental effect on the vigor of couch grass.

Ridding the garden of horsetail and ivy
The Mexican marigold (*Tagetes minuta*) will restrict the growth of horsetail and ivy though it may do little for the color scheme of your garden!

A poor old widow in her weeds,
Sowed her garden with wild flower seeds.
Not too shallow, not too deep,
And down came April, drip, drip, drip.

And now all summer she sits and sows,
Where willow herb, comfrey, bugloss blows.
Teasel and tansy, meadow-sweet,
Campion, toadflax and rough hawksbit.

WALTER DE LA MARE 1873–1956

KEEPING SPREADERS IN CHECK

Fresh mint is a delicious herb to grow in the garden, but unfortunately it will spread like wildfire once it gets going. It will totally overrun the vegetable patch or herb garden, much to the detriment of everything else growing nearby. Solve this problem by planting mint in an old trough, bucket or sink that has been buried up to within one or two inches of its rim. This is an excellent method for curtailing the spread of most rampant herbs and flowers. Take care, though, to ensure each container is well watered during dry weather.

Like a chamomile bed –
The more it is trodden,
The more it will spread.
TRADITIONAL SAYING

RELIEF FROM PLANT STINGS

Stings from nettles and other plants which exude acid poisons can be alleviated by an application to the skin of an alkali solution. The most effective are onion juice, tobacco water, wood ashes, dock (*Rumex*), tomato and potato leaves.

When your fingers nettles find,
Be sure a dock is close behind.
TRADITIONAL RHYME

CLEANING A GREENHOUSE FLOOR OF MOSS

Take equal parts of fine coal ash from the fireplace and ordinary cooking salt. Mix together and scatter this on the moss-ridden portions of the floor and then sprinkle a little water all over. Leave for two to three hours, then sprinkle with water again. When the floor is dry, brush with a stiff broom.

CLEARING SCUM AND WEEDS FROM PONDS

If left unchecked, blanket weed (filamentous algae) can choke an ornamental pond. A simple way to remove the weed is to take an ordinary bamboo cane – the type used for staking your beans and insert the cane in the pond where the weed is thickest, revolving and pulling the cane at the same time. The blanket weed gradually becomes attached to the cane like spaghetti to a fork. Keep turning and pulling until you have a good load on the end of your cane.

Another easy and most proficient way of ridding a pond of green algae and weeds is to send in the ducks. They will clear it completely, but there is always the risk that they may remove more aquatic growth than you intended.

REMOVING TREE STUMPS

To avoid the laborious effort required to remove stubborn tree stumps, try this harmless "scientific" method. It takes a little time, but it certainly dispenses with the need for mules, chains or heavy machinery. Bore half a dozen holes, about one inch in diameter and twelve inches deep, in the top of the stump. Half-fill the holes with saltpeter and top up with water, then drive in wooden pegs to seal them. Three months later drill out the pegs and repeat the process. After a few months, remove the pegs again and top up the holes with paraffin. Allow the paraffin to soak into the stump, topping up the level several times as necessary. Light a fire on top of the stump and watch it gradually but surely smolder away.

SALTPETER (Potassium nitrate)
A colorless or white crystaline compound
used in gunpowder and fertilizers.

Cut thistles in May, they grow in a day;
Cut them in June, that is too soon;
Cut them in July, then they die.
TRADITIONAL RHYME

CHAPTER SEVEN

FOLK AND FABLE

"The Greeke writers of husbandry (and after them Plinie, and the worthy Neapolitane Palladius Rutilius) report, that those seeds may be preserved in safety from all evil and garden Monsters, if the bare head without flesh, of either Mare or she Asse (having been covered with the Male) be buried in the Garden, or that the middest of the same be fixed on a stake set into the earth, be erected."

FROM THE GARDENER'S LABYRINTH *BY THOMAS HILL BORN 1529*

GARDENERS FROM TIME IMMEMORIAL *have indulged in varying degrees of* MAGIC *to achieve good crops and prevent* — FACT AND FABLE — *pests and disease. Sometimes, the fine line between* — FACT AND FABLE — *meant that superstitious beliefs were reinforced by successful results. In reality, the successful results were due to natural laws that were simply misunderstood and were not, of course, being influenced in any way by* OCCULT OR MAGICAL PRACTICES. *Some of these practices survive into our own times, but the majority have long been abandoned.*

WASHING HANDS BEFORE PLANTING

The Romans insisted on holding hand-washing rituals wherever they planted certain plants, a custom which later came to be reserved almost exclusively for tree-planting. In the absence of such a ritual, the tree would have a poor start in life, be prone to disease, and remain infertile.

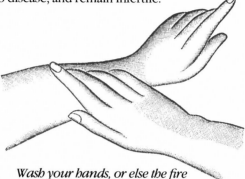

Wash your hands, or else the fire
Will not tend to your desire.
TRADITIONAL RHYME

COLOR TRANSFERENCE

During the sixteenth century it was thought to be possible to change the color of fruits. Holes were bored into apple trees with an auger and a solution of water and the required color was poured in and the holes sealed with wax. Peaches were grafted onto red-damask plum trees to produce red fruit. Red roses were grown next to apple trees to turn the crop red.

Likewise the same process was applied to tastes so that by grafting a branch from a sweet-tasting fruit tree to that with a sharp taste, the resulting fruit would have a dual tang. Soaking bulbs in wine to induce purple fruits was a technique practiced by the ancient Romans.

PLANTING UPSIDE-DOWN APPLES

One curious belief entailed the planting upside down of apple seedlings in the hope that the apples themselves would form with no cores. Similarly, flowers were planted upside down to alter their shape, form or color.

If apples bloom in March,
For fruit you may search.
TRADITIONAL SAYING

CELEBRATING FIRST FRUITS

The old custom of celebrating the first crop of vegetables or fruits from newly planted trees still occurs in some parts of the world. This practice took various forms. Often each member of the family would taste the crop in the belief that otherwise the harvest would rot.

TALKING TO PLANTS

It is surprising to learn just how many people today regularly talk to their plants, both indoors and in the garden. Gardeners in the Old World thought nothing of encouraging their plants along by an affectionate word (or with a good reprimand if they refused to grow and produce the required flowers and fruit). Modern research has proved that plants do actually respond favorably to sound stimuli from either speech or music, which proves that both our ancestors and those of us who still indulge in the practice today were, and still are, not as stupid as might first appear.

TAKING PLANTS FOR A RIDE

To induce plants to produce double flowers it was once common practice to dig them up and wheel them around the garden in a barrow. This was done at regular intervals until the flowers appeared.

WRITING TO RATS AND MICE

Gardeners once employed a novel method to rid their gardens of rats, mice, ground hogs (woodchucks) and moles. They wrote polite letters to the creatures, inviting them to leave their gardens and placed the requests in their burrows. This practice is thought to have originated in ancient Greece where farmers, anxious to clear their gardens of mice, wrote messages to them offering alternative accommodation.

GROUND-HOG DAY (February 2)
According to legend, ground hogs emerge from hibernation on this day. However, if they see their own shadows they return to their burrows – a sure sign of a late spring.

HALF PRUNING

Some gardeners even today are reluctant to prune fruit trees and bushes drastically. Their belief is that half the bush must be left for the birds. In earlier times plants were only half pruned so as to "cherish the sap" and as an appeasement to the plants themselves for having to prune them at all.

HAMMERING NAILS INTO TREES

This was a common practice in both America and Britain. Iron nails were hammered into fruit trees so as to increase their yield. This would bring "lazy trees to their senses", though most likely it was to inhibit the tree's sap flow. Sometimes nails were driven in to keep witches out of the orchard. Another curious habit was to whip trees to induce them to fruit better, this being done ritually on Good Friday.

GARDENERS' TOOL LORE

The superstition that garden tools, particularly a spade, must never be carried indoors by the gardener is one that was prevalent in the South and in parts of England's West Country. The belief was that the sharp edge of the tool would "cut down" the fortunes of the household. Similarly, to lay a rake on the soil with its teeth uppermost was thought to increase the likelihood of a bad harvest or the gardener's ill fortune. Black slave workers of the old South believed that any gardener leaving a hoe standing upright in the garden at the end of a day's work would be unable to sleep that same night.

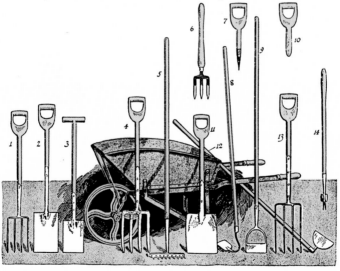

For if in your house a man shoulders a spade,
For you and your kinsfolk a grave is half made.
TRADITIONAL RHYME

PLANTING BY MOONLIGHT

Gardeners used to say that fruit trees planted under the radiance of the new moon would always provide an abundant crop. They supposed that the fullness of the moon's light created a warming effect and consequently orchard trees like peaches which came into blossom at night would never be damaged by frosts. This particular belief has its origin in a more ancient age, for Varro, writing on the subject around 36 BC, wrote: "Trees which are planted in a row are warmed by the sun and the moon equally on all sides, with the result that more grapes and olives form, and that they ripen earlier".

THE MOON

It is a wet month to be when there are two full moons in it.

*When the ring (halo) round the moon is far – rain is soon,
When the ring round the moon is near – rain is far away.*

*In the old moon (waning moon) a cloudy morning bodes a
fair afternoon.*

*A full moon bodes fair weather.
A clear moon, a frost soon.*

TRADITIONAL SAYINGS AND RHYMES

USING MOON PHASES

All seeds of plants that bear foodstuff above ground – fruit and nut bearers, salads and herbs – should be planted in the first and second quarters of the moon.

All seeds of plants that bear foodstuff below ground – root vegetables, tubers, ground nuts – should be planted in the third and fourth quarters of the moon.

DAY-OF-THE-WEEK PLANTING

This attitude to planting is still observed in parts of North America, mostly among gardeners of the older generation. Certain days of the week are considered either good or bad, depending on their significance. Fruit that is picked on Sunday was believed to return to the tree the minute it was picked. Friday was a very bad day for planting, being synonymous with Good Friday and the crucifixion. There was a general taboo applied to gardening on Sunday – anything planted on this day was destined to die prematurely.

NORTH-TO-SOUTH PLANTING

Just like those gardeners who sowed by moonlight, other Old-World gardeners sowed and planted by starlight; the light here coming principally from the brilliance of the Pole Star. They planted in rows running from north to south, partly to align with the radiation from the Pole Star, but also to ensure, quite practically, that plants acquired an equal amount of sun on either side.

Dating back to Roman times, compass points have played a significant role in planting. Virgil tells of:

> *Some Peasants, not t'omit the nicest care,*
> *Of the same soil their nursery prepare,*
> *With that of their plantations, 'lest the tree,*
> *Translated, should not with the soil agree*
> *Beside, to plant it as it was, they mark*
> *The heaven's four quarters on the tender barks,*
> *And to the north or south restore the side,*
> *Which at their birth did heat or cold abide.*
> *GEORGIC* BY VIRGIL 70–19 B.C.

MODERN RESEARCH at the Agricultural Research Station, Lethbridge, Alberta, Canada has discovered that the roots of cereals and other plants eventually align themselves to a north-south axis, and germination of seed sown to this axis is significantly improved.

SEX, FERTILITY AND PLANTS

Indulging in sexual intercourse among crops was a custom which occurred frequently in many places throughout America and Europe. Ritualistic copulation was so performed to increase the fertility of plants.

Sometimes pregnant women were employed to plant seed, the inference being that their own obvious bountifulness would transfer itself to the growing plants. Similarly, pregnant women hugged trees to induce healthy growth.

If lavender grows well in the garden,
The girls of the house will miss on marrying.
TRADITIONAL SAYING

POLLINATING TOMATOES

Procure a cotton ball or some other similar light fluffy ball and tie it to a stick. At about midday, treat every tomato plant by lightly touching the front part of each flower with the fur. This will distribute the pollen, fertilizing the female organs of the flowers.

If you enjoy the fruit, pluck not the flower.
TRADITIONAL SAYING

BLOOMING OUT OF SEASON

This once widespread superstition with its gloomy prediction of death involved certain plants whose flowering season was restricted to a certain time of the year. Thus if they bloomed out of season, the worst was feared. Gardeners in the Midwest regarded a second crop of flowers on cherry trees with great apprehension, while in Britain it was normally the out-of-season flowering of pear and apple trees that caused alarm. Other flowers which were dreaded in this way were white roses and violets (*Viola*).

A bloom on the tree when the apples are ripe,
Is a sure termination of somebody's life.
TRADITIONAL SAYING

GREEN THUMBS, GREEN FINGERS

In America it is said that a successful gardener has "green thumbs", while in Britain they are said to have "green fingers". Those poor souls who lack for gardening skills are said to have digits that are either purple, black or brown. The worker who possessed the greatest "green thumbs" was always elected to make the first planting and sowing in a field before the rest of the labor joined in. Gardeners, even to this day, believe in having a close affinity with their plants, which may well be the source of all "green thumbness". In fact the renowned plant breeder Luther Burbank once said that love was the prime nourishment a plant needs. It is fitting to note that during the 1906 San Francisco earthquake, when much of the city was destroyed, not one plant or one pane of glass from Burbank's greenhouses was harmed.

CHARM SIGNS AND CROSSES

To save their crops from witches or those purported to have "the evil eye", gardeners combined pagan symbols and Christianity to provide charmed protection. Small crosses made from the twigs of rowan and birch, both pagan trees of good fortune, were placed in seedbeds to counter any witch's spells that may have been cast. Sometimes a circle was drawn round the garden with a hazel twig as an act of protection, though for this to have total effect the twig had to be cut before sunrise on May Day. In Europe, many years ago, peasant farmers protected their crops by ploughing a cross into each of their fields at springtime as soon as planting and sowing had been completed.

WASSAILING THE FRUIT TREES

In Britain, where fruit orchards were commonplace right up to the early twentieth century, "wassailing" was an annual custom whereby good health to the trees and encouragement to fruit well was celebrated early in the New Year, usually on January 17 (Old Twelfth Night). In recent years the custom has been reintroduced, especially in the great apple-growing region of Yakima, Washington. In the cider orchards of Somerset, England, even to this day the largest apple tree is toasted and cider is ceremoniously thrown over its trunk.

Wassail the trees, that they may beare,
You many a plum and many a peare;
For more or less Fruits they will bring
As you do give them Wassailing.
ROBERT HERRICK 1591–1674

AS BIG AS MY BUTT!

Seed sowers in the Midwest still compare parts of the human
body with the desired size of crops. Such comparisons are
usually concerned with the head, arms or thighs. Gardeners
visiting their root crops recite rhymes such as:

As long as my arm
As thick as my wrist.

As they recite so the tops of the plants are shaken to empha-
size the point. When sowing cabbage seed the incantation is:

As round as my head
And as big as my butt!

While for turnips they recite:

As round as my head and as big as my thigh,
And some for the neighbor who lives close by.

TRADITIONAL RHYMES AND SAYINGS

PLANTING BIRTH TREES

This lovely custom, which has made a comeback in recent
years, used to be widely practiced throughout the world in
one form or another. On the birth of a child, a tree is planted
that same day. From then on both child and tree share the
same birthday. In Switzerland, during the nineteenth century, a pear tree was planted for a girl and an apple tree for a
boy. In Israel, newly born boys had cedar trees planted on
their birthdays. In the past, trees planted on these occasions
were closely watched for any signs of ill health. It was supposed that should the tree grow healthily, the child linked to
it would similarly grow in health, but if the tree ailed in any
way, somehow the child would ail too.

MAKING A PLANT TOTEM

To the Native American Indians there is a subliminal network between all forms of life that allows an interchange or interaction to take place between them. They use totems as sensors to tap into this network so as to allow communication between the human, animal, vegetable and mineral kingdoms. With this in mind, each person, depending on their date of birth, has a plant particular to them. A cutting or twig from this is cut and then decorated with items such as paper, ribbon, feathers and beads, and then placed among the flowers or vegetables in the garden. From then on, whenever you walk in the garden, you simply concentrate on your totem and this brings you into spiritual contact with the plants in your garden.

Plant Totems (Birthdays)
March 21 to April 19: Dandelion
April 20 to May 20: Wild clover
May 21 to June 20: Mullein
June 21 to July 21: Wild rose
July 22 to August 21: Raspberry
August 22 to September 21: Violet
September 22 to October 22: Ivy
October 23 to November 22: Thistle
November 23 to December 21: Mistletoe
December 22 to January 19: Bramble
January 20 to February 18: Fern
February 19 to March 20: Plantain

Show me your garden and I shall tell you what you are.
ALFRED AUSTIN 1835–1913

CHAPTER EIGHT

WEATHER OR WHETHER?

A Gardener's life
Is full of sweets and sours;
He gets the sunshine
When he needs the showers.
COMPENSATION *BY REGINALD ARKELL 1882–1959*

GARDENERS *have always been* AT THE MERCY OF
THE ELEMENTS *which is why our*
forefathers were so acutely aware of THE WEATHER.
Nature herself is a fine weathercock and provides us
with many clues as to what kind of weather to expect,
BE IT FAIR OR FOUL. *Much traditional knowledge of*
this kind originated in the Old World long before the
introduction of modern WEATHER FORECASTING.

FROST COATS FOR PLANTS

For plants that are tender and susceptible to frost damage, some form of protection is necessary if they are to survive severely cold conditions. Provided the plants are not too large, make frost jackets to cover them and keep them sheltered from frost. For plants no more than one to two feet tall, place wicker, rush or cane baskets upside down over them. For larger plants, construct a cage from either wire, bamboo canes or twigs tied together with strong twine. Stretch canvas or some other thick material over the cage and tie it in place. Stand the cage over the plants when frost is forecast.

PROTECTING PLANTS FROM SHORT SPRING FROSTS

During spring, short sharp frosts often occur towards dawn. Protect plants from this type of frost by giving them a cold-water shower from a garden sprinkler during frosty weather. The finer and more mist-like the spray, the better the effect.

MAKING PLANTS MORE RESISTANT TO FROST

It is known that both potassium and sodium minerals which are found in organic matter can lower the freezing point of plant sap. Therefore, keeping plants well nourished with compost, manure and wood ash will build up their frost resistance. Extra protection can be ensured by spraying the foliage with an infusion of Valerian (*Valeriana officinalis*) during those evenings that precede nights when frost is expected.

SAFEGUARDING YOUR BROCCOLI IN WINTER

Take a spade and remove a little of the soil from the north side of each plant. Then on the other side, insert the spade gently and lever the plant over until its head inclines towards the ground and faces north. By doing this the sun is prevented from shining directly on the broccoli heads. This stops a bad frost turning plants brown by allowing any thaw to occur slowly.

PROTECTING WALL TREES AND SHRUBS FROM FROST

Many tender fruits and ornamental shrubs and climbers are grown against a sunny south-facing wall. Problems arise with the arrival of winter frosts which can seriously damage or even kill plants overnight. One easy way to protect wall plants is to hang an ordinary curtain rail above the plants, along the length of the wall, so that you can drape net curtains over them. At night, when frosts are likely, pull the curtains across to afford perfect protection, and draw them back again during the day.

After a frosty winter there will be a good fruit harvest.
TRADITIONAL SAYING

PROTECTING FRUIT TREES FROM FROST

An unexpected heavy frost in spring will often ruin a fruit tree in blossom. When the weather forecast is ominous, keep your trees warm at night by providing them with a fire. A really dedicated gardener might stay up all night to feed a bonfire, but it is more convenient to place a brazier (the sort you burn your garden cuttings in) in the center of a group of three or four trees, and light a coal fire. The fire may not last all night, but the brazier and ashes will stay warm until dawn.

"If the careful Gardener would withstand the force of frost approaching, then let him burn store of chaffe if such plenty be there or near at hand, but for lack of the same, may he use the dry weeds plucked up out of the Garden or Field, and the bigger Thistles, or other waste fruits in many places of the same, especially toward that way which the wind bloweth, for on such wise handled, that the evil nigh or at hand is adverted."
FROM *THE GARDENER'S LABYRINTH* BY THOMAS HILL BORN 1529

PLANTING OUT OF SEASON

Normally it is inadvisable to transplant shrubs and trees during periods of severe cold when the soil is in an unreceptive state for planting. However, it can be achieved successfully if the plants are "puddled-in" using hot water instead of cold. This, strangely enough, does no harm to the plants' roots.

Much February snow,
A fine summer doth show.
TRADITIONAL RHYME

KEEPING PATHS CLEAR OF ICE AND SNOW

Clearing paths after a heavy fall of snow can be a tiresome chore, especially if there are many to clear. To make life easier, scatter a liberal coating of salt mixed with sand over the paths before a snowfall. Mix a pound of salt with every three or four shovelfuls of dry sand, and ensure that the entire surfaces of paths and drives are covered. Snow will not settle on this mixture, thus saving much time and effort.

PREVENTING CONCRETE FREEZING

To prevent newly laid concrete paths freezing in cold weather, lay sacking (or plastic sheeting) over them and spread a layer of earth or sand on top to act as an insulant.

ERECTING WINDBREAKS

Salt-laden winds play havoc with coastal gardens. Few plants, with the exception of carnations and pinks (*Dianthus*), thrive in salty air and it can be difficult to enjoy the sun if there is a strong prevailing breeze. The simplest solution is to plant a hedge of evergreen trees or shrubs, but our forebears took it a stage further by erecting fences of woven hazel twigs (hurdles) on the windward side of the hedge.

If the wind comes from the west on October 12th,
a mild winter follows.
TRADITIONAL SAYING

ROOT-PRUNING WINTER GREENS

Sometimes the late growing season is very mild and wet which encourages greens to produce an over-abundance of leaves. To retard this growth, plants must be root-pruned during early fall. This involves chopping round the plants with a spade, about one foot away from the stems. On each cut, the blade must be inserted to its full length. This prevents sappy growth and helps to prepare the plants for winter.

St Swithin's Day (July 15) if it do rain,
For forty days it will remain.
TRADITIONAL RHYME

ST SWITHIN was the Anglo-Saxon bishop
of Winchester, England between 852 and 862.

PROTECTING PLANTS FROM FOG

This method works best in enclosed or sheltered areas such as in a cold frame, cool greenhouse, or walled garden. Fog can adversely affect tender and half-hardy plants, but if you place one or more saucers containing a little household ammonia in the enclosed environment, the plants will survive even the worst "pea souper".

Mist in March, frost in May.
TRADITIONAL SAYING

WATERING DEEP-ROOTED PLANTS IN DROUGHT

The problem with watering a deep-rooted plant during very dry weather is that unless the ground is thoroughly soaked, allowing water to seep down deep into the soil, the roots will grow towards the surface and be prone to severe scorching. This can eventually lead to the death of the plant. One simple but extremely effective way round this dilemma is to sink a couple of feet of one-inch metal or rubber piping in the ground next to a newly planted tree or shrub. Leave an inch or so of pipe projecting above ground. When really dry weather comes, simply place a funnel in the top end of the pipe and pour in a bucket of water. This will go straight to the plant's roots where the water is most needed.

NATURE'S SUN SIGNS

When swallows fly high.
When dew lies abundant on the evening grass.
When a raven is seen in the morning soaring very high in circles and croaking with a hoarse sound.
When beetles fly in the evening.
When bats are seen flying in the evening.

TRADITIONAL SAYINGS

PROVIDING SHADE FOR NEWLY SET PLANTS

If you shade newly set plants for two or three days, their survival rate and growth will be greatly increased. Shade can be provided under boxes, cartons or old discarded flowerpots. If these are not readily available, use large leaves such as those from bracken or rhubarb.

STONE MULCHES FOR DROUGHT CONDITIONS

Long periods without rain, particularly during hot weather, can cause serious long-term damage and eventually kill many plants. Constant watering is often necessary in these conditions, but during severe droughts there are usually water restrictions that prohibit the use of a garden hose. Mulching plants is one line of defense to reduce evaporation from the soil and using stone pebbles is one of the most effective methods. They can either be gathered from soil in the garden or purchased from a builders' store as washed marine pebbles. For mulching purposes the stones are laid one next to the other in a circle around each plant; the amount of mulch for each plant depending on its size. For larger shrubs, roses and young trees, the stones can be laid in several layers to increase the effectiveness of the mulch. Pebbles must be removed when the drought is over as bugs and germs will begin to colonize on them to the detriment of plants.

Exceptionally hot weather during the first week in August foretells a cold, hard winter.
TRADITIONAL SAYING

BIBLIOGRAPHY & ACKNOWLEDGMENTS

**The author and editors
gratefully acknowledge the following:**

A Countryman's Day Book, C. N. French *J. M. Dent & Sons*
A Garden Treasury, Elizabeth Blackall *Simon & Schuster*
Art For Commerce, E. S. & A. Robinson *The Scholar Press*
Cassell's Domestic Dictionary 1885 *Cassell, Petter, Galpin & Co.*
Collected Green Fingers, Reginald Arkell *Herbert Jenkins*
Country Fair Magazine *The Aldworth Press*
Country Wisdom, Jerry Mack Johnson *Jerry Mack Johnson*
Four Hedges, Clare Leighton *Victor Gollancz*
Gardener's Magic, Maureen & Bridget Boland *The Bodley Head Ltd.*
Homestead Hints, Donald J. Berg *Ten Speed Press*
How To Enjoy Your Weeds, Andrew Wynne Hatfield *Frederick Muller*
Keble's Christian Year 1827, Rev. John Keble *Cassell, Petter, Galpin & Co.*
Old Wives' Lore For Gardeners, Maureen & Bridget Boland *The Bodley Head Ltd.*
The Book Of The Home (4 Volumes) *The Gresham Publishing Co.*
The Country Calendar, John Claridge, Shepherd *Sylvan Press*
The Country Gardener's Almanac, Martin Lawrence *Main Street Press*
The Forgotten Arts: Herbs, Richard M. Bacon *Yankee Books*
The Gardener's Folklore, Margaret Baker *David & Charles*
The Gardener's Labyrinth, Thomas Hill *Oxford University Press*
The Gardeners' & Poultry Keepers' Catalog *William Cooper*
The Heirloom Gardener, Carolyn Jabs *Sierra Book Club*
The Home Owner's Manual *George Newnes Ltd.*
The Montgomery Ward & Co. 1895 Catalog *Dover Archive*
The Romance of Animal Life, Rev. J. G. Wood M.A. *Isbister & Co.*
The Sears, Roebuck & Co. 1908 Catalogue *Dover Archive*
The Vegetable Garden, MM Vilmorin-Andrieux *Ten Speed Press*

LAST KNOWN PUBLISHER/IMPRIMATUR *PRINTED IN ITALICS*

*The following poems, extracts and illustrations
are reproduced by kind permission of:*
A WIDOW'S WEEDS BY WALTER DE LA MARE
The Literary Trustees of Walter de la Mare and The
Society of Authors as their representative. Page 74
THE LAND BY VITA SACKVILLE-WEST
Copyright Vita Sackville-West. Reproduced by permission
of Curtis Brown, London. Page 43
EXTRACTS FROM THE GARDENER'S LABYRINTH BY THOMAS HILL.
Published by Oxford University Press. Pages 10, 16, 18, 77, 91
SELECTED WORKS FROM GREEN FINGERS & MORE GREEN FINGERS BY REGINALD ARKELL.
Published by Random Century Ltd. 1956. Jacket and pages 23, 32, 33, 55, 89
JACKET ILLUSTRATION FROM FOUR HEDGES BY CLARE LEIGHTON
Published by Victor Gollancz Ltd. 1970.

*In the name of the bee,
And of the butterfly,
And of the breeze,
Amen.*
ENVOI *BY EMILY DICKINSON 1830–86*

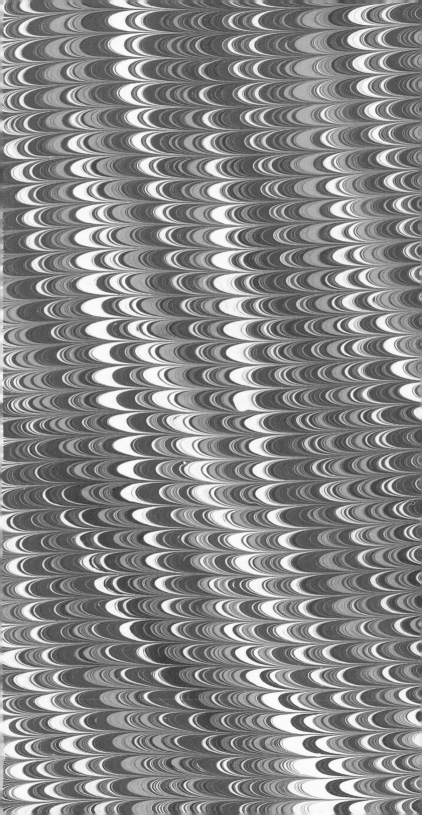

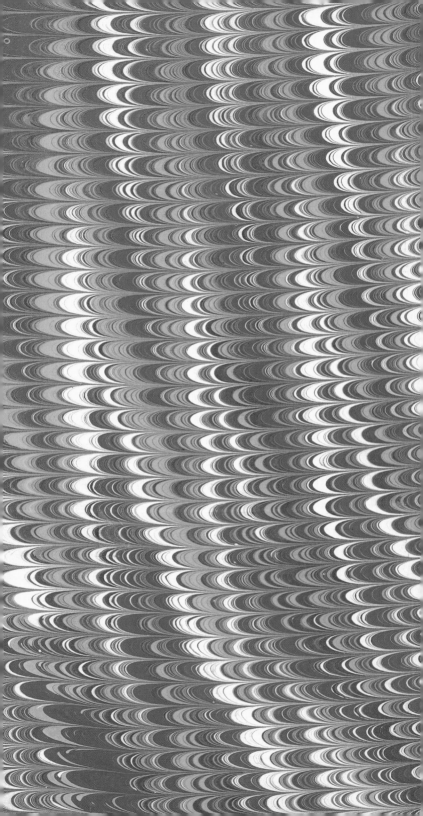